The Ultimate Agile SCRUM Master Certification Training

SADANAND PUJARI

Published by SADANAND PUJARI, 2024.

Table of Contents

Copyright 1

About 2

Introduction 3

Why You Need To Take This Book 6

The Professional Certification: What Is It? 11

Objectives 17

What Is Agile? 23

The Foundation Of Agile 30

Agile Principle 01 34

Agile Principle 02 37

Agile Principle 03 40

Agile Principle 04 42

Agile Principle 05 & 06 46

Agile Principle 07 50

Agile Principle 08 53

Agile Principle 09 57

Agile Principle 10 59

Agile Principle 11 62

Agile Principle 12	65
Why We Use Agile Part 1	69
Why We Use Agile Part 2	74
Agile Frameworks	81
Introduction To Scrum	86
The Scrum Guide	91
The Scrum Values	95
What Is The Scrum Flow	104
Product Definition	111
The Scrum Team	118
The Scrum Plan	124
The Sprint Plan	136

Copyright

Copyright © 2024 by **SADANAND PUJARI**

All rights reserved. No part of this book may be reproduced, scanned, or distributed in any printed or electronic form without permission. Please do not participate in or encourage piracy of copyrighted materials in violation of the author's rights. Purchase only authorised editions.

The Ultimate Agile SCRUM Master Certification Training

Learn , Understand; Experience The SCRUM Framework And Become A Certified Scrum Master!

First Edition: Jun 2024

Book Design by **SADANAND PUJARI**

About

This Book is for anyone who wants to rapidly improve their career prospects in the booming industry of software development without learning how to code. It is also for anyone who wants to make the most of their Development Team, improve their management skills and create higher-value products for their business.

If you are an entrepreneur with an idea, this Book will teach you how to manage a team to turn your vision into a reality ready for the marketplace. After taking this Book, you will have a good understanding of the skills necessary for effective leadership as a Scrum Master and be well-prepared to take Scrum Master certifications.

Until now, you might have struggled to manage a team to build the right product or solution. Or, you might have finished a project and the item developed was over budget, delayed and once launched it didn't get as many users as you hoped. If this sounds familiar, then this Book will help!

Anyone who is looking to build a career in Scrum Management must understand the above. If you don't, then this Book is perfect for you. Go ahead and click the enrol button, and we'll see you in Chapter 1!

Introduction

This Book is focused on a key, agile framework that we use to achieve agility in the business world, and that framework is scrum. This is the best scrum Book there is because it is derived from over 20 years experience working with agile in the software development world. Hello, my name is Andrew Black. To date, I have taught over 18000 students in both the corporate world and in the academic world, both remotely and face to face. In this Book, I will be your teacher, your coach, your guide, your mentor to give you a brief biography of myself. I have moved through many aspects of the business world.

I began my career as a junior computer programmer and moved through the ranks and spent my final eight years in the corporate world as a senior national I.T. director. I currently function. Within my own organization as the CEO, it's a consulting practice, and I am indeed a consultant and as a lead consultant, I function as an agile transformation specialist. By that, I mean, I coach, I advise, I teach and I lead many, many teams who build software development projects, as well as senior management groups who want to learn about agile in an organizational structure, all to understand how to function successfully with this as well.

I am a lead professor in the academic arena in the university arena. I teach only at night, five nights a week because I teach professionals who work in the daytime and come back to improve their skills and to improve their positions within their organization to learn about this particular area. So after 20 years of teaching, I have gained many insights and refined the concepts of teaching so that you can assimilate the knowledge that I am delivering and produce and understand from that knowledge. I created this Book for those who want to excel in the world of agility and product development and organizational leadership. So what that said, by the end of this Book, you will have all the skills, knowledge and ability and understanding required to achieve your scrum master certification.

The one we're looking at is the PSM one, which is the professional scrum master certification that comes from scrum board run by one of the co-founders of Scrum Ken Schwarber. You asked the question, What are you going to teach us that will actually help us to do this? Well, we are going to journey through the 2020 scrum guide put together by Scrum Board with a partnership between Ken Schwager and Mr. Sutherland. Jeff Sutherland, co-founders of Scrum and we will drill deep into the nuances and depth surrounding that guide. We were going to learn and teach you about where to use scrum, how to use scrum, when to use scrum.

Because Scrum will differ from organization to organization and from team to team within an organization. We will learn about the ceremonies as scrum, what is around those ceremonies, how we do them, what the responsibilities are. We will teach you about the roles of Scrum again. What are the functions within those rules? You will learn about the differences between project management and project leadership. You'll learn which one actually works in the agile world and which one does not work in the natural world. You will learn what agile teams, how to create performing agile teams, and you will learn much, much more in this Book.

As we wrap up, I'd just like to state this that many of the major corporations and companies around the world are using Scrum. We bring up names like Microsoft, Amazon, Intuit, Salesforce, many of the hundreds of thousands of corporations and companies using Scrum. So to make yourself attracted to them from a position of hiring or working or increasingly improving within that organization, you need this Book. The Book will turn you into a skilled user of scrum with a deep understanding of the free world. So what are you waiting for? Jump into the Book and we will see you online. Thank you.

Why You Need To Take This Book

And welcome to the studios of the online Agile Mastery Academy, our vision, a world achieving success through the agile philosophy. Our mission to get there, to transform you, the student into a passionate, agile person is experiencing success. And welcome to our Book, the scrum master class, or as I like to say, scrum the master class. And the question that we like to ask as we begin this chapter is why the scrum framework, why should you learn about scrum? That is a critical question. And what we want to tell you about learning about Scrum is this. First of all, there are many companies that are using scrum today. So if you want to achieve success in any vocation, it's a good reason to do it. And looking at the different organizations that use scrum, let's look at some of the industries globally that scrum is being used in.

We'll find it in the financial services industry, places like banks, mortgage companies, lending organizations or areas like the food and beverage major across our globe today. And then we have the medical devices, vocational area, medical devices and legal and consultancy. My consulting practice is very, very agile. We use scrum hospitality. The hotel industry, the restaurant industry and the customer support industry scrum is being used in all of those industries. Continuing on construction? Yes, construction minus many of my students have been in the construction, world travel and tourism, education, data, data analytics, telecommunications, insurance industry game. I find this a big one in the insurance industry.

Other industries that we have as well, we have the pharmaceutical industry, the government agencies, the automotive industry, the engineering industry, transportation and in our list here finding manufacturing. So this covers a wide spectrum of organizations globally that are using scrum. Let's zero in on a few of the companies that will use scrum and are using scrum. Who are some of these companies? What are they? Well, let's take a look. We've got companies like big names Google. Apple. Facebook, yeah, Spotify, Adobe, you'll hear about the Spotify way of doing things in the agile world. Airbnb, Bank of Ireland, Amazon, HSBC, Salesforce, Netflix and still continuing on, we have legal Ryanair, three M, IBM, Deloitte, Siemens large organizations.

And the reason I list these large organizations is because so many times my students come to me and they say, well, agile is good. If you're doing a small startup, agile is good at a small company. Yes, it is. It works super in those areas, but it also works very well in large organizations. And I can give you and will give you during the Book some anecdotal evidence of some of these organizations and what they've gone through to achieve agility. For example, Microsoft, Salesforce, Siemens, we can talk. We'll talk through some of those. So these are some of the companies that you find that are using agile. So if you look at the industry and you look at the companies, the question is why should you? Why should you learn scrum? Well, let's talk about it.

What did scrum allow you to do with your projects? Well, they'll do this. And I like to start off by saying this. You need to learn scrum because you will be able to work and build adaptable products. The process is adaptable. Scrum processes are designed to embrace change. And if you've gone through our Part two, part one and Part two of Agile, which is our foundational philosophy, teaching the foundational philosophy, you'll find that agile is all about adapting to change. The scrum allows you to do that. It is customer centric. There's an emphasis on having a collaborative approach, and this collaborative approach brings your customer onto your team.

Your collaboration with your customers on a daily basis is value delivered, the prioritized product backlog process, which we work on through with one of our ceremonies that we will learn about. This ensures that the highest value comes to the top of the list. We set priorities and just those priorities on a daily basis. We include continuous feedback. Scrum is about continuous feedback. Jeff Sutherland, co-founder, says this, and you will hear Jeff a number of times through this Book. But Jeff says this scrum, it's all about the feedback loop. Without the feedback loop, you can not be agile. So feedback from customers is received daily throughout the whole process to our standard ceremonies.

Another reason that you need to learn scrum is because it gives you transparency. It's a scrum with all of its ceremonies that we allow us to have. What we call invisible information radiators allows us to have our scrum boards burned down, always in front of the team and in front of anybody. That, for example, comes into a team room where we are transparent to the entire organization. It allows us to build trust, which is essential for scrum teams. Without the trust, you cannot have an agile team. Agility is not, is not available without trust, and scrum allows us to have that trust because of the transparency and the collaboration that we've talked about. It creates a high trust environment. It allows us to have continuous improvement of the products that we are building.

We have this what we call the ceremony, the backlog grooming that allows us to keep on reprioritizing, going back and looking and improving what we have done in the past. It allows us to maintain a sustainable pace again, go back to the principles of the agile manifesto. And we see that that is a principle that we maintain. This pace and scrum processes are set so that people involved can work at a pace that they can sustain indefinitely. So these are some of the reasons why you should learn about this group. This is what it will help you to do in your project. Work on the product building that you are working on. So as we wrap it all up in this particular chapter, we asked the question again why the scrum framework? Why use the scrum framework? Well, there's a very easy answer that encompasses everything we've talked about, and it is this scrum equals success.

That's what it's all about. We want to be successful and scrum worked with a full understanding of the agile philosophy equates to success. Yes. That is why I emphasize with my students. You can come in and learn about Scrum, but you won't understand agile unless you learn first. Agile philosophy is the foundation of everything, every one of the frameworks, and we talk about frameworks such as extreme programming, feature driven development. Christel SDM. We can talk about the scaled, agile frameworks safe nexus, less scrum of scrum skilled scrum. They all focus on scrum. And that understanding of scrum requires you to understand agile, critical critical foundation. So if you haven't learned it before you take this Book, go back and take it. My Book is part one in part to understand the agile, agile philosophy. So with that said, thank you for listening to this and continue on through Scrum The Masterclass. We will see you online. Thank you.

The Professional Certification: What Is It?

And welcome to the studios of the online Agile Mastery Academy. And welcome to our Book scrum, the master class. Before we get into our material, we've already talked about why you should take it, but what I want to do a little bit of a focus on is something that I've talked about in a couple of the earlier chapters and that is the professional scrum master one certification. From Scrum Dawg, what we call the home of Scrum. And this is Ken Quavers organization, Ken Schwager is one of the co-founders of Scrum. And what we are attempting to do in this Book is we are attempting to prepare you to take. The professional scrum master was certified, and that's our focus, our focus is to lay groundwork, to give you an understanding, work through what we call the scrum guide and allow you to get this PIM one certification.

And we've read this, or we will read this again in the Book, but the exam is for five provided by Scrum Dawg and contains 80 questions. There are single choice questions. There are multiple choice questions and true or false type questions. You will have one hour to complete the exam and to pass the exam, you need to score 85 percent. You must get at least 68 questions right out of the 80 on the exam. So I wanted to cover that, but there's something else I really want to talk about. When we talk about this PSM one certification, I'm going to give you some information that some of the subject matter experts in our world talk about. When they talk about the PSM one, it is the most meritorious sort of certificate of all that certified scrum and is the professional scrum master PSM by scrum board. In addition, there are more reasons to like this certificate than just this one here, and that's what I want to talk about. I want to talk about some of these reasons. Now here's one.

Let me read it. Other certifications you can easily get by attending a class or getting it through an exam where failing could only happen by intention. The PSM assessment requires good knowledge of the original version of Scrum and its passing requirements, as I mentioned, are high 85 percent. Such stringent criteria to obtain the certification provides more teeth to its certificate than the other similar notifications provided in the marketplace, and I have a few of those other certifications I have this year, Sam and a few others as well. But I like the PSM will be one or all three PSM one percent to 10 percent three. Now here are other reasons why this is a good certification.

It is administered by a company guided by Ken Schwarber, who is one of the co-founders of Scrims. We've talked through that. It does not require any mandatory training Books, and that is my concern with some of the other certifications, no matter what. You know, how much experience you still have to spend upwards to 2000 or so dollars to take their Book. One or two day Book just to be able to write the exam. I don't think that is a very good thing to do, and the PSM assesses the knowledge on authentic scrum. So it's always focused on what we call authentic scrum, and its fee is nominal. One hundred and fifty one hundred and fifty dollars USD to write the exam. Other reasons: After paying the fee, the password for the assessment is sent to a registered email, usually within a business day, and the password does not have any expiration date.

The assessment can be taken from anywhere with a computer and internet connection, and once you acquire the certificate, you do not need to continually pay more money and renew it like some of the others that I have. And there are no prerequisite qualifications for the assessment. You can take it without knowing anything about Scrum. You will pass it, but you will and you will lose your one hundred and fifty dollars because you don't know anything. But there are no qualifications. You can take it when you feel you're ready to take it. Now, one of the things I really want to stress here and this is a big one. I am an educator, both in the corporate arena and as well in the academic arena, in the professor, in the university arena.

So I can tell you that when you have to write exams, there are different types of thinking that you have to do. And what I want to stress here is this As we look at scrum, it is an agile framework. Scrum is a framework and both can. And Jeff was stressed that it is not what we would call a methodology. A prescriptive methodology and what that requires is you to think differently as you prepare for these types of exams. A methodology and I have created and built some in my time. It's very different from a framework. So let's talk about it. Let's talk about this different way that you prepare. So you're ready when before you even take my Book what you have to think about as you prepare to take your piece and one.

So with that said, let me say this when you're looking at getting certified with the methodology, for example, navigators out there, we've got the old SDM 70, we've got things like an exam. These are some of the ones out there now. If you know anything about those methodologies, they contain numerous, numerous volumes of information. Why is it because they tell you what to do, everything to do and how to do it? It's all laid out for you. The checklists, the template. It's all there for you. So if you spend your time studying and studying and studying like you would a university Book and then you write the exam, you can pass it, but you haven't done anything with it. Where a framework is different, it is not a prescriptive checklist. It is a pattern.

And within that pattern, you're going to adapt in many different situations. And I think Can puts it well when he said the intent of Scrum is not to tell you what to do, but to point out where your process is broken, where it's not working well, and that comes to the surface very quickly. So when you're preparing for the exam, as I've talked about and I will talk about throughout the Book and we will continually flow through the 2020 scrum guide. It's a 13 page guide, but it contains all the theory that you need to know about Scrum, but it doesn't tell you how to do everything. So what you need to do is you need to understand the theory, but not just scrum. And we cover this. In the first part of this Book, you need to understand the agile philosophy.

So when you have questions on the exam and many questions are scenario based, how would you deal with this? What would who would who would deal best with this on your scrum team when you have this situation? What should you do here now? It'll all be based on the theory that we talk about in the scrum guy, but it won't be questions that come out of this scrum guy. This is all based on this scrum guy. That's why you need to spend the time in these Books understanding and going through them over and over. That is my intent with our scrum Book to give you that material that you can walk through over and over. Understand what we're saying and begin to think in your mind.

How would I handle this here? How would I handle this situation using the scrum theory now as well when we get to the end of my Book? I have guided you towards the scrum org open assessment, a spot where you can actually write some of the practice tests and they guide you through it. They tell you what's right, what's wrong and why. And I always tell my students this, go through those and keep going through them until you score 100 percent. Don't stop. Go through them. If you do it once every day for five days until you score that, 100 percent do it as well. I have included at the end a series of practice tests and the same thing. Now mine is the ones I include are not the ones where you click and hopefully get this right.

I'll show you the question. I ask you to pause the Book and think it through and think what you think your answer would be. And then you turn the Book back on and then I tell you what the answer should be, and I tell you why and why the other ones are not right. And we go to the scrum guide. So I go through a fair amount of explaining and that's again part of the learning process. But you begin to see, OK, these are different scenarios, and this is how I would apply the scrum theory here. This is how I would wear the scrum. Artifacts would fit in here and how I would use a scrum artifact here and doing this. All of these things should rise to the surface as you begin to understand the theory and then learn through the practice test how you might or how you will have to answer questions on the certifications.

So we're doing everything possible to help you pass your PSM one certification. It is prestigious in our industry and I believe. Or I shouldn't give a number, but I think we're around thirty three hundred thousand so far globally in certifications with the same one. But you need to know your material. So that's what I'm emphasizing here with the scrum master class. We're going to help you. We're going to help you work towards that. That's our intent. So we wish you all the success. So keep that in mind. Keep that as your dream here. The same one. So thank you very much and we will see you in the Book.

Objectives

Welcome to the studios of the online Agile Mastery Academy. I always like to start off with our vision. The academy vision is a world achieving success through the agile philosophy. Our mission to achieve the vision is to transform you, the student into a passionate, agile person experiencing success daily. That's what we are about, and to do that one of the Books we have is what we are beginning here, which is scrum the master class. We want to delve into this area, drill in and see what's really happening. Our focus is on studying the scrum framework, and I will mention this a number of times during the Book, the scrum is not a methodology. Agile is not a methodology. The definition of a methodology, and I have created them in my career, as I talked about in the intro chapter.

A methodology is a prescriptive way of doing things within an organization. And we've learned since the late 1980s, as the methodologies began to crumble, we learned that the methodology would not address the needs of the product. Building in my area was information technology, why our world had become very volatile, not that it wasn't volatile before, but it was with technology now that linked everything together. And as things changed on a day by day, week by week, month by month basis, our traditional ways of building products no longer worked. When we delivered the product, it was obsolete. It was not what the organization needed. So we're going to study the framework. We'll talk about the framework. So how are we broken this Book down into a couple of chapters?

And what we've done with each chapter is we've created a series of chapters. You'll see chapter breaks and we begin a new chapter as well. Within the chapters, you'll find that I will have some topics. And the reason we've done it this way is that I have learned through all my years in the academic arena that you don't want to load too much knowledge onto an individual because the retention that we have within our brains will fill up. And then once we fill it up, what comes in does not retain. So I will give you a short piece. My intent is for you to sit back and think about it, go back and review that piece to make sure you have full understanding as well. I recommend something that I do with my classes in school as well as in the corporate arena.

Take note, take notes and some of the things that we're going to be talking about. So with that said, let's hit the pre Book chapter. This first chapter is going to be what we say is the pre Book, and we're going to look at our Book introduction. And just before we jump into it, I always like to start off by saying Thank you, thank you for taking your time to take in this chapter. And this Book is I know how valuable your time is, and time today has so many things that pull on it on an ongoing basis, many distractions. And for you to sit back and take the time to do this requires me to say thank you. But more than just that, thank you. I want to give you a big thank you. And with that, I also want to congratulate you on taking the time and taking the risk to start working through this Book.

I appreciate it, and I will do everything in my power to allow you to learn and understand what this is all about. So let's begin by doing a quick Book. Overview This will give you an overview of the Book before we start, and we're going to look at the learning objectives. These are the learning objectives that I have for you. So first of all, we're going to give you an agile refresher. The objective here is that you understand agile. I know some of you have taken my two other Books that I have as a start for this in the sequence. Agile one, part one and agile part two. But some of you haven't, and I'm going to be very strong on this. If you haven't, I would recommend you do it. Why? Because whatever we do with any framework in the agile world requires us to have knowledge of the foundation.

You can have a scrum shop and I am called into some to help them figure out what's going wrong because they are achieving no, no results that you would achieve in a successful, agile organization. And very quickly, I point out to them, you haven't built your foundation on agile. You're using Scrum as a predictive methodology, and it won't work. So understand agile. Everything we do in scrum is based on the agile foundation. You need to understand that we will give you an overview of that. At the beginning of the Book. We will give you an overview of Scrum and will show you the traditional way of operating and building a product and the scrum way so you can actually see the differences.

And that way we can work off of it. And then we're going to take in the scrum values from the agile, not the agile manifesto about the scrum guide for 2020. We're going to start off by looking at the scrum values as everything we do in the scrum perspective. The values are set upon the four value pillars from the agile manifesto that I just mentioned. So in our scrum guide, it's tied into the agile manifesto through our scrum values, and we're going to look and talk to those once we've done that will then give you a definition of scrum that will define it and talk that through looking at the co-founders and what their definitions are. And we will hear from one of the co-founders a few times as we walk through this. Co-Founder Jeff Sutherland. And then we'll dive into a detailed scrum breakdown.

We'll go into the depths and we'll explain the whys and wherefores, explain the hows and. I'll give you pointers and tips and hints of what I've experienced in the industry, some things you won't find anywhere, even in the scrum guide. And I'll point those out to you and then we'll delve into the scrum ceremonies and look at each one. How do we do it? When do we do it? What are the results? And we're going to surprise you because we're not going to talk about scrum ceremonies. We'll talk about six scrum ceremonies, and I will explain that when we get to the chapter. Moving on with our Book objectives, we are going to talk through the deliverables from a true scrum process, the framework.

What are the key deliverables that we should be delivering from the process? And then we'll look at the scrum team when I work through with my classes, when I work through with the corporate arena. And I mean, as a scrum trainer and as scrum coach, one of the things I emphasize is the foundation of scrum. One of the key foundational principles of Scrum is a performing scrum team. And how many performing scrum teams do I see in organizations that call me in because of problems? Very few. So we talk about that, we'll explain that then we'll talk about the scrum rules. We'll explain to you the key rules, the scrum, and that's where I'll explain to you this whole role of the leader in scrum versus the manager at scrum, what works and what doesn't. Then we'll work through that.

And then as we wrap it up, we'll talk through. As we've gone through, all these parts will wrap it up in the scrum theory. What can Schwager and Jeff Sutherland have defined and written up in their guide? The theory behind Scrum and how all of these parts fit together? And then once we've done that, we'll talk about the results that you should be achieving. With Scrum in an agile process, using the agile philosophy if you're not achieving those results. Then the process is broken and you need to fix it. Plain and simple, we're finally going to wrap up with a scrum conclusion, and part of that conclusion will be looking at what so many people are interested in is professional certification, and we're prepping you, preparing you for scrum dot org.

The professional scrum master one cert. This is the certification, the first level, and you will have the knowledge and the understanding by the time you've gone through this Book and and you've studied through the scrum guide and we'll talk about that, you'll have a copy available to you in the Book as well. At the end of the Book, I will have a series of practice tests available for you. They won't be only unlocked when you have completed the Book. So let me read to you about this certification, the PSM one, the professional scrum master level one exam is provided by scrum dot org and contains 80 questions. There are single choice questions, multiple choice questions and true and false types of questions. Those are the three types you get on the exam.

You have one hour to complete this exam to pass it. You need a score of 85 percent, which requires you to get at least 68 of the 80 questions correct. So we're going to prepare you for that. We're going to give you examples of that. So that is our Book that you are about to embark on journeying through with me as your conductor, as your coach, as your lead is your guide. I will go through that with you. So that ends our first chapter, which is what we call the Precor chapter. So again, go through it, make sure you have a good understanding of what we're going to cover in the Book. And then once you've done that, then I will see you in the next chapter. Thank you.

What Is Agile?

And welcome back to our Book scrum, the master class. We've completed the first chapter of our Book, which was the freak, what we call the precautious chapter. Now we're moving into chapter one, which is about agile and is the agile refresher portion of the Book. We're going to move into that, and I do want to emphasize, as I've emphasized earlier on, that to understand how scrum actually works. First of all, you need to understand agile. Scrum is founded upon agile, we've emphasized that and to have a good understanding and success in scrum, you need to understand the foundation. So we're going to do a quick refresher and we're going to do an agile review. We're not going to do the in-depth Book that I have parts one and part two, parts one and two. We're going to have a quick refresher from those, just an overview.

And if you haven't taken them, as I've said earlier, then I would recommend that you go back and take those. Those are your foundation, that is your foundation. Agile is the foundation for whatever you're going to be doing. So we want to do a review of agile, and this is less than one of the reviews. There's going to be a few chapters from the review, so this one is going to be explaining to you what is agile. So let us go through that process now, as I always like to do when I talk about what agile is, I always begin by setting context or what I like to say leveling the playing field. If you are outside of North America, you would probably understand soccer or what you call football, and that has to be on a level playing field in North America.

We have North American football or American football, and we do that. We want a level playing field, so everybody gets the same chance. Well, that's what we want to do in this Book when we explain agile. And to do that, first of all, we tell you what agile is. Not Agile is not a methodology, and I will continue to emphasize that there is no agile methodology. A methodology is a prescriptive way of doing things. It's a formula. It is everybody following the same step by step process, and if they do, they will be successful. That's not agile. Agile is an adaptive way that changes from company to company, from team to team within a company. So you need to understand that we'll talk about it. It is not just about information technology.

Most people think well, when we refer to agile, we're referring to programming. No, it's not about information technology and it's not a silver bullet. In other words, it doesn't mean that you have to. For example, if you're building software products, you use agile for every product. Some were better in the development process if you use what we call the traditional waterfall way. Yes. I emphasize that some products work better in a waterfall way of working, we'll talk about that. And again, it's not a way of programming, it's not about it and it's not a way of programming. So let's delve into it. So what is this thing that we call agile? Well, it's two things. And one comes before the other, and the first thing is agile is a way of thinking, it is a way of how we think. In other words, it takes place between our ears. That's not the process we follow.

It's how we think. Let me explain that there's an understanding required from us as we go into this arena of agile. And there's something that takes place in our brains and you hear this in our neuroscience labs and you hear the term neuroplasticity, and I won't delve into the details behind it because I've studied that. But what the bottom line equation that comes from this arena is that knowledge, which is what I'm giving you here, does not equal understanding. I'm going to help you understand the knowledge as we walk through it. Understanding is where success comes from. So you might have a head full of knowledge, but you need to understand it. And many times understanding comes by doing it. So we'll talk about that.

So what this way of thinking leads to is a totally different way of working. That's the big part here. This is a way that is diametrically opposed to how our traditional organizations operate. You know, those hierarchical everybody looking to the top way of operating? Well, we don't operate that way in the agile world. We'll talk about how we do operate, so what agile is, is a philosophy. It is a philosophy, not a methodology in the Cambridge English Language Dictionary. This is what it says. The philosophy of a subject is a group of theories and ideas related to the understanding of that subject in agile. There is a group of theories and ideas, and we fit those together to understand how it works, and it differs again, as I've emphasized from organization to organization and from team to team within an organization.

So what this tells us, it is not this prescriptive methodology. This prescription, if you have a headache, you go to the doctor, the doctor says, take two pills every six hours and then after four days you will be fine. So we do the same in our traditional methodologies. If you follow all of these steps, when you come to the end, you will have a successful product. Well, no, that is not what happens. So it's not a prescriptive way of operating. It is an adaptive way that we operate. We continually adapt our frameworks to fit into how agile is working in our organization. So it's not this checklist that everybody follows the formula driven way of operating. It requires a shift in the mindset. It requires our organizations to think differently. We talk about an organizational cultural shift. This means it has to come from the very top.

When I go in to train an organization, the first thing I am asked to do before I train any part is that I'm in the information technology industry. Before I train any part of the team, I need to sit down and train the executive. It has to start at the top. If they don't understand agile, I don't care how the team operates at the bottom, it will not work. Plain and simple. So you need this organizational cultural shift. I know some of you may disagree with me, and that's fine. I don't I don't get annoyed at that. But this is my experience in 20 years. That's many organizations. If you go over to my own academy website, you'll see the logos of many, many companies I'm working with. So the definition of agile is let's come up with a definition and we're going to use the definition that comes from Mr. Jim Highsmith, one of the signers of The Agile Manifesto.

One gentleman who has his own agile framework. He gave us this definition. Agile is the ability to both create change, create change and respond to change in order to profit in a turbulent business environment. This is change that takes place during the building of the product not changed. The product is going to cause change in the organization, but change takes place as we're building the product continually week after week, having to adapt here, adapt here, change here and change here. And Jim says agile teams thrive when this change begins to happen. Why? Because they know they are on the right track. Now, another gentleman I like to use these two definitions is Scott Ambler.

Scott was the original key architect behind rational rows and the rational, unified process from rational. And then, as they moved over to IBM, IBM purchased them. Scott was with them, but he soon slipped away because he realized this was not an agile way of working. And Scott got into the agile arena, and he came up with his own way of operating. And if you're a data monitor process modeler, you've got to read his works. He's all about agile modeling, but he's come up with a framework called It's a scaled, agile framework. We'll talk about skilled, agile frameworks differently. It is based on scrum and is called disciplined, agile. Originally, it was called this discipline agile development.

Or you may have heard of D & D. Now it's just the way, and it has been purchased by the Project Management Institute as their key framework of choice. So he laid it out this way. Agile. Is the use of an iterative and incremental or what we like to see this evolutionary approach to software development, in other words, you don't build software, it evolves out of the process. It's an emerging product that you're building and is performed in a highly collaborative manner by self-organizing teams with just enough ceremony that produces high quality software in a cost effective and timely manner. Why? To meet the changing needs of its stakeholders and understand here, I underline the changing needs of stakeholders during the building of the product.

So our traditional way of doing the product is when we come along and we have created this four month process of putting together all the requirements and getting them signed off and for the next two years, building those requirements. And when we deliver the product, the business says we're not there anymore. We've changed. We've got new executives, new ways of operating new things. We've purchased new businesses, we've got new products. We need to be able to adapt to that on a continual basis. So agile, agile is all about change. Change is the key word and more than just about change. It's all about us embracing change. We want change because change means we're on the right path. That's what it's about. So as I've got here, we desire change all the way through the project.

The day we start, we're looking for change to take place because we're beginning to understand what it is and we create change. We create change all the way through our project. So that's what agile is about. We create this change by continually inspecting and then adapting. And in scrum, you'll hear me talk about the sprint. This is the constrained time increment that we use to produce a piece of working software no more than four weeks, but usually we recommend one to two weeks. And what happens at the end of that time frame? We inspect our stakeholders, inspect what we've built, and then they say, Well, no, we should change this and add this, and we adapt and then we build and then we expect and then we adapt it. We fix, then we inspect, then we adapt it.

That's what our process is all about. So that ends this chapter in chapter one, our agile introduction, if you want to call it that. And again, I recommend going back through it. Listen to what I say here. So you understand the meaning of what we're dealing with and what the impact is within your organization. And again, as you listen to this and you think, well, I really need to know more about this, I recommend you take part one and part two of our Book. With that said, thank you very much for spending the time in this chapter, and we will see you in less than two of chapter one. Thank you.

The Foundation Of Agile

Welcome back to the studios of the online Agile Mastery Academy and welcome back to our current Book scrum master class. We're now going to be moving into the third chapter of our chapter one on agile. And in this chapter, we're going to be looking at the foundation of agile. We always talk about the foundation, no matter what we build in real life in our world, around us. As we build it, it must be based on a foundation. As things grow, they are based on a foundation, a root structure foundation, no different with our philosophies and our frameworks. They all maintain and all contain the foundation. So our foundation for agile that we're going to look at is this.

We have something called The Agile Manifesto put together in 2001 and Snowbird Utah by 17 people that came together to come up with this foundation of agile after frameworks had been coming into existence, they wanted to bring it all together and set upon a foundation, and they came up with the Agile Manifesto, which began with this statement. We are uncovering better ways of developing software by doing it and helping others do it. Well, that's really a motherhood statement that we have said over the years. I know in all my years we've focused on this just wasn't working. But this is the difference this next line says through this work, we have come to value and what we have come up with are what we call the four value pillars of agile. Everything we do sits upon these pillars.

If you have problems in your organization with agile. Look at the value pillars and I'll guarantee you you'll find one where the wage structure is wrong. So here's what we have with our four pillars: individuals, people and interactions. People and how they work together has greater value than processes and tools. If you've been in our industry as long as I have, you know, we have put our focus on the processes, the methodologies and the tools that we use to help us work with those methodologies. That's not where it is in agile. It doesn't matter what process or tool you use. How are people working together if they're not? There's a problem. We need to fix it. We need to focus on that. This is what both Jeff and Ken Schwager say. Scrum does not tell you how to do anything. What it does.

It points out to you where the gaps are in your organization or, as Ken Schwarber says, it points out very quickly where you're screwing up, in his words. So we need to make sure that it's not about the processes until we value the people. The people are what build software, tools. Computers do not build software, so that's value pillar number one value pillar number two is our focus is on working software, not spending a year building a pile of documentation, mountains of documentation, a great big requirements report, a logical design report, physical design report, our process model report, our data model report, our test strategy report, all of these reports and we haven't still started even building the key product that we're supposed to build, which is our software.

So software working software, now there's the key there. It's not just software. The software has to be working user acceptance testing software. That's where the value is, and we start building that as quickly and as soon as possible. Third value pillar customer collaboration over contract negotiation. So what does this mean? Well, we walk into an organization where we're a vendor, we build software, we get our contract signed and we build. Three years later, we delivered it and the company is no longer there. They're gone. Very. Everything's changed. The software is useless. So we say, yes, we have a contract, but we build our contracts in such a way that as we collaborate with our customers, their business environment is continually changing.

We're adapting and we've built our contracts to that. And yes, we can do it because I do it. Finally, the fourth value pillar responds to change over following a plan. Now let's put something here that I really emphasize and that a lot of people get messed up with this statement. They think, Well, we don't plan. No, it should really say this. It should say responding to change over just following a plan, you see there's more planning in the agile world and you see that with our scrum process, there's more planning than our traditional waterfall way of planning. But you see, we continually plan, we plan daily, we plan by Sprint, we plan by release that we're continually adapting those plans as the world around us is changing. So those are the four value pillars we have now.

I want to emphasize this with this particular statement. While there is value with the items in white, we value the items in green more. Yes, there's value with processes and tools, there's value with documentation, there's value in working with contracts and there's value in plans. But the higher value is in the green parts of those statements. So keep that in front of you at all times and. Those four value pillars hold up the 12 principles of Agile. Everything we do in scrum must meet those four value pillars and at least one of the 12 principles, if it doesn't, then throw it out. That's what it's about. So we're ending this chapter or third chapter in chapter one. Go back. Review it. Make sure you understand the foundation. Dig deep. Set it in there. Understand it. And once you've done that, then we will see you in the next chapter. Thank you.

Agile Principle 01

Welcome back. To the studios of the online Agile Mastery Academy, and welcome back to the next chapter in our Book scrum the masterclass. What we're going to be doing in this particular chapter in less than four is we're looking at the 12 principles of Agile that we wrapped up talking briefly about in our last chapter. We're now going to delve into the 12 principles. These are critical for us to know for our foundation. And what we're going to do is for each principle, we're going to keep it in chapter four, but I'm going to break it into a series of small chapters that we like to call topics. So topic one is going to be agile principle one. So let's talk through it. Let's look at what this principle says. It says this is our highest priority. Is to satisfy the customers through early and continuous delivery of valuable software.

So the question is asked: why continuous delivery? Is it because we just want to get our customers the software as quickly as possible? Valuable software? Yes. And then no, we want to get the value or we want to get it to them quickly. Why we like to put it this way, it allows us to do this. We want to fail fast. Phil, early. And Phil wafted, Wow, we're talking failure here, it was all of success. Well, understand that in most things in our life, success comes from learning from failure. Fix that and you get success from that. Prime examples. Most of us, if not all of us, have at one time or another left the Earth and flown in an aircraft.

And the two gentlemen, the Wright brothers who built the first aircraft, failed numerous times and crashed their machine before they were able to actually take off and do that short flight that shook the world and went into our history as the first step in our air flight. The history? But they failed fast, they wanted to fail as fast as they could, and they wanted to do it early and they wanted to do it off. And why? Well, we put it this way. Tom Peters said that we test fast to fail fast, so we adapt fast. But let me wrap it up or put it a little stronger from Tom Pearce, he said this way. In his book In Search of Excellence, he said that we want to fail fast so that we learn fast and then we fix fast. So that's what our mandate is in the agile world. We want to fail as soon as possible.

So the sooner we produce a piece of working software, our customers will say, no, that's not exactly what I want. So then we can fix it from what we've learned in the discussion and then let them see it again. So that's why we want to produce software early and as quickly as possible, so our customers are stakeholders, the users of our software tell us, will this meet their needs? Now understand we've always done that in our traditional developments, but we've waited till the end of the project to do our U80, our user acceptance testing a two year project with a team of 300. And we do that and everything breaks.

One thing breaks. And because that system, that massive system has been put all together, one thing breaks. It requires us to fix 300 other things because of our integration. This way we do a small piece. We fix it. We tie it all in together, and we can move very quickly and give the customer exactly what they need when we're finished. So that is where we end up with principle one, and I'm going to stop the chapter here and then we'll move into principle number two. Thank you very much, and we will see you in that topic. Thank you.

Agile Principle 02

And welcome back to the studios of the online Agile Mastery Academy and welcome back to our Book scrum masterclass. We're currently working through chapter one and chapter number four, which includes the 12 principles of Agile or the 12 principles of the Agile Manifesto we've currently worked through principle number one. Now this is our second topic because we're breaking the principles into topics. Topic two is agile principle number two. What is this principle? This principle is laid out simply this way. We welcome changing requirements even late in development. Agile processes harness change for the customer's competitive advantage. Why do we want to continually adapt and accept change? Because the customer is in a competitive environment and when their competitors change, when the environment changes around them, they need to change. For competitive advantage.

So our whole focus is on adapting to the world around us. So we welcome these changing requirements. And the question I get asked so many times is why? Why don't we just go with this large group of requirements that we began with at the beginning of the project and build that? That's great. But when we deliver that product, everything has changed around it. The world has changed. We talk about the fact that we are shooting at a moving target. We have a target. That target has been set in our business case at the beginning of the product. The project and that product target within a month or two months is no longer there. And if we're not changing our Book and adapting to that, we're not going to be able to be where we need to be when we deliver the product.

Because when we get there, it's like shooting an arrow when the arrow arrives. There's no target where the target is moved 50 feet down the range. It moved as we were shooting the target or shooting the arrow. So here's what we talk about. We always need to adjust our Book daily, and this is what agile is about. It is about continuing, continually adjusting your Book and most of it being derived from the continued change in the business world around us. This is what we don't want to end up like. We don't want to sink our project. Why? Because we went off Book. So we're continually looking at correcting our Book. We have economic changes in our world. We're going to that right now.

As I record this Book, we're going through a pandemic which has changed the business world dramatically globally and has changed the economy globally. So if we're building products, we need to adapt to that so we can actually deliver a product that's going to meet the company's needs in this time. We have things that the government changes. The government sets new tax rules and sets new rules for accounting. It comes out of our government organizations and the government changes. We have elections and we have a whole new government, maybe a different party going into government, which has different ideas, and we're in the middle of building a product which is impacted by those ideas. We need to change the product.

So when we deliver it, it is what the customer needs. We have the business changing around us. Our business changes. We have different ways of operating. We have new products that we're putting out. We've purchased another organization. We need to adapt to that or we have personnel changes. We have a new executive team that is coming in or a new CEO or a new CIO or a new CFO. And we're building products in those areas. They have different ideas. So we may in most cases, will have to adapt the product as we're building it to the new way of working. And then we have our global changes. Economies change. Even though I talked about economic changes, we're going through as I explained our global change.

Now we need to adapt the product Book to meet that global change. So that's what we're focused on. So instead of heading in one direction and not shifting Book, we need to be like this. We need to be able to turn on a dime. We need to be able to change the direction, changing requirements. Our Book changes. Plain and simple, and that's what we're about, the faster we can shift our Book, the faster we bring our project project in line with the ever moving target. It is that moving target that we're focused on. So that ends our topic to our principal too. And we will move on to agile principle three in the next chapter. Thank you. We'll see you there.

Agile Principle 03

Welcome back to the studios of the online Agile Mastery Academy and welcome back to our core scrum, the master class. We're currently moving through chapter one chapter number four, and we've broken it down into topics. We're looking at the 12 principles of agile and what we've done is we've taken each principle as a topic. So we're now hitting topic number three, agile principle number three as we're going through the agile manifesto. So let's look at agile principles. Three, What does it entail? What does it cover? And what we talk about is our intent is to deliver working software frequently from one to four weeks with a preference to the shorter time scale.

So if you recall in principle number one, our focus is to deliver software early, working software early and how we enforce that is through this principle by building it in specific small increments no larger than four weeks. But our preference is for the shorter time scale. Why? Well, if we do a four week piece of work, it's not going to be one piece of work is going to be a number of and I'm going to use the term we use as scrum. We'll talk about it using stories. We have maybe chosen seven eight nine uses of stories to do in that four week timeframe when we come to the end of the four week timeframe and there are problems with the customer.

So that's not exactly what I need. There's more work for us to fix, and it takes longer than if it was only a one week segment, one week segment, a small piece of work. It's easier for us to adapt to adjust it and fix it without looking in, building all those, fixing all those other things that have been integrated because they hadn't been integrated yet. So that's our intent with the shorter timescale is faster for us to move through the process. So keep that in mind. And again, I want to bring up this statement that we brought up in our first principle: why do we want shorter time frames? Why do we want to keep them short so we can fail fast and learn from that failure and fix fast? We want to fix it as quickly as possible. So keep that in mind.

Our intent when we're doing this is to get this from the customer. We want to hear a yes, you're right on track and we keep on moving or no, and we're happy with a no because it means we can keep our ship on Book, our project on Book and slightly adjust our trajectory by learning what is not actually correct in that piece. So it's a thumbs up or thumbs down every week, every two weeks. I never let my teams go longer than two weeks. I find that fits the best. So that's it for this particular topic. Topic three Principle number three, go back through it. And then once you make sure you understand it, let's move out into principle number four, which should be topic number four. We will see you there. Thank you.

Agile Principle 04

And welcome back to the studios of the online Agile Mastery Academy and welcome back to the continuation of Scrum, the masterclass and where we are right now is we are in this chapter one of the Book, which is what we're dealing with an agile overview and we're in chapter four, where we are looking at the 12 principles of agile and what we've done is to break it down and have these segments very short. So you don't have to absorb a whole lot, but we can explain each principle. I have set each principle up as a topic, so we are looking at agile principles. Number four, this is topic four in the chapter four series. So let's take a look at what this principle says.

Principle number four says this business, people. And developers must work together and daily throughout the project. Now this has been a real issue over the decades in the information technology industry software development. What we have done is we have segmented. We have broken our organizations into two parts. US and them. Our society, the development group and theirs is the business, so we've had this adversarial approach and you'll find many organizations, most of the business despises the information technology group and the opposite is true. They do not operate as one. And you know what happens when there is division, when there's division is failure. It's an old song that we used the same way back in the 1960s and that was united. We stand and are divided.

We fall, and it's very true from a team perspective. So how do developers and business work together daily, not monthly or not? Once a year daily, every day we're working together and we do that within our teams. It's the team approach that we take and keep this in mind. A team does not have, well, we have a sub team. There could be sub teams in sports teams, but in the agile world there is no sub team. We'll look at that when we look at that within the scrum guide, it's emphasized there is one team and one team. Only every member on that team is part of the team. So as we like to say, business and IT are one team, not two separate groups within the team, but we are one team, all one team and all the entire team needs to play to play together to win.

So our teams train together when I do training in the agile world, when I train teams, I ensure that the product owner is within every class. They have to be part of it. They're part of the team. They have to understand what is going on. Then once the teams have trained together, they work together daily. They work together. And I emphasize that we do not have silos within our teams and I've been coaching some organizations over the past year outside of North America, in both Europe and South America. And I'm finding so many of them say, Well, you know, for this ceremony, only the developers are involved. And for this ceremony, we will invite the product owner and this ceremony with the scrum master.

Well, that's not a team. You don't put a sports team on the field and say, well, let's take, for example, American football. You don't put the sports team on the field, say, well, for this game, the quarterback won't be there. It's foolish, and it's foolish in the agile world to say, well, the product here is not going to be a part of this ceremony in the daily scrum. Every member of that team is there, and I have enforced this since the when I began working with agile teams in 2003. And I know I went against the grain, but every day, every day, a daily scrum. It's amazing. The product owner gives such insight. If they see things a little bit differently, they listen to what each member is saying, which is what I did yesterday. This is what I will do today. And these are the impediments.

And it's amazing how many times the product owner at the end will say, you know, you can get rid of that impediment just by doing this. So it is that collaboration that has to take place between all members. And it is painful in some cases for old school I.T. individuals practitioners to take on that approach. My business member that is across the table is not an adversary. They're part of my team. So it does take a mindset shift in scrum. The product owner owns the product backlog. Let me say that again, the product owner there called the product owner for a reason they own the product backlog, which means they can do whatever they want to that product backlog, they can change priorities, they can change priorities hour by hour. They can add new things. Take things.

That's their prerogative. They own the product. They own the product backlog. We'll talk about that one. They are part of the team. They attend all meetings. And I have said push back for two organizations who are failing. And I have walked in and I have said what I want for the next three retrospectives. I want the product owner there. Well, the punishment can't be there, they're the business. No, they're not, they're the team. They're part of your team. They need to be on that team. And it's again, it's amazing the insights I get from product owners who are sitting around in that retrospective and they clear things up so quickly. They see things that we don't see. And then we see things that they don't see. So that's why we're a team, so I keep that in mind. It is the team that makes this particular principle work. You work together daily with business and business is part of your team.

So that's it for this particular topic and this principle IN principle for. Go back through it and listen to what I'm saying and please, I know I will. We'll get pushback. But this is from 20 years of experience, and I'm going to say this in 20 years, I have not had one project fail. Because I've used these principles and when I say failure, we have three principles or three criteria that we measure success on every project of mine has been a success. Every project has come in on time, on budget. The third one is that it's given to the customer more than they ever expected. Every time. OK, with that said, thank you so much. We will see you in our next chapter.

Agile Principle 05 & 06

Welcome back to the studios of the online Agile Mastery Academy. And welcome back to our Book scrum master class. We are in our first chapter of the Book, which is looking at an agile refresher, which is our foundation. Agile is the foundation of what we do in scrum. So without understanding, the foundation scrum will fill in your organization and I'll be blunt about it. We are in chapter number four, and in this chapter, we're looking at the 12 principles of agile, we're not looking at the detail behind them that you'll find in my agile Book parts one and part two, you'll find the detail there. So what I've done is I've segmented this to keep each of the chapters short. I've segmented them into topics and we are in topic five. But here I have included both Principal five and Principal six in this topic.

So let's talk through principal number five first, and let's look at what it says. It says that we build projects around motivated individuals. It's important that the individuals that are on the team can work in this environment and are motivated to work in this environment. You have one bad individual on a team. It pulls the entire team down. When we talk about teams, I'll talk about this, but we call these people barnacles. And the reason we do is when you have a boat in the water. I live on the west coast of Canada, and what happens to the boats that are in the Pacific Ocean is over time they gather on the bottom. These little things called barnacles, living creatures that grow and what they do is they slow down the boat because they are in the boat. It's no longer smooth on the bottom.

This is what happens with individuals on teams that are not motivated to be on the team. They slow the team down. So what we do is what you would do in a real life situation with barnacles every couple of years you go and raise the boat and scrape off the barnacles. We do that with our teams. We scrape off these people, we get them off the team because they slow down the team, so build projects around motivated individuals, give them the environment and support they need. Give them exactly what they need to run this. Make sure that they have a team room. Make sure they have all the facilities, the tools available. That's the environment. And then the business says we support you and your decisions. You see, the team is autonomous. That is the key point.

And we'll talk about that when we get down to the team aspect of scrum. It is an autonomous team. But above all, business must trust them to get the job done if the trust isn't there. You can forget about success in an agile world in scrum. The team must be trusted and we'll talk about trust a little bit later. I have an entire Book on agile teams and we deal with the fact that we need to have trust. And I explain how that works and how the scrum master is responsible for doing that. And I give tips and different ways to actually achieve this quickly. We'll do that in that Book. So again, we need people who are motivated to work in this environment. We give them the support and whatever they need in that environment to make it successful and we trust them to get the job done.

So that's principle number five that we have. Let's move to principle number six. Principle number six says this. The most efficient and effective method for conveying information to and within a team, a development team. An agile team, a scrum team is face to face conversation. Now be careful with this one. Many people think that it has to be physical face to face, and that's not true. We are currently living at a time, and most of you who read this will have been in this time frame in 2020 and 21, where we have this SARS-CoV-2 pandemic and many businesses have gone remote. Many, many teams are operating in a remote way and the scrum where absolutely it works. She still can have face to face conversation.

In my other academy that I have, I have another academy other than the agile one, I have Books. I have an entire Book on Zoom. I have an entire Book on Microsoft Teams. These two tools allow you to have face to face conversations continually. One of the tools I use is Slack. Slack is a collaboration tool that you can link Zoom into. You can link Google Docs in to have all your communication, all you're sharing, all your collaboration, all your chapter calls, all your chapter meetings, all in one spot, all located in one platform. But this is where you can have face to face conversation continually. You set up your Zoom meetings and the people are there.

So keep that in mind face to face conversation, don't fall away from that and then have, well, we'll get together on the phone in a week's time. You're going to fail. You will fail. If you do that, you need these meetings and we talk about this as this continual meeting face to face. We meet continually, face to face. We have six scrum ceremonies. Yes, I know many people and we have four. We have six. And we'll talk to those in these Books. We prefer co-location when we're physically meeting or working. We all have co-located teams. But when we're remote, we can't be co-located, but we are remotely located.

Pair programming, pair programming doesn't work remotely. It's a little more difficult, but it still will work and we will cover that. And technology allows us face to face no matter what situation we're in. So keep that in mind. This is what we're looking at in this particular principle. Six And these are the principles that make agile work. If you, I think Kent, back of extreme programming, laid it out this way, you need to have all of the 12 principles in place. Without all of them, one will fail. Because they're all flawed to a certain extent, but you need all of them in place for it to work effectively. So keep that in mind as you go through this. So thank you very much for sitting through this chapter and we will see you in the next chapter.

Agile Principle 07

Welcome back to the studios of the online Agile Mastery Academy in our Book scrum, the master class. We are currently journeying through chapter one, which is our agile refresher, and we are in chapter four, which covers the 12 principles of agile. We've gone through six of them now. So weird topic six because we included two in Topic five, so topic six, we're looking at agile principle number seven. So let's go into this and let's see what was written down many years ago when the agile manifesto was put in place. What this principle stated. It says this. Working software is the primary measure of progress. So if you're in a software development project working on a software development application, you measure your progress by how much working software you have created.

So how is this different? Well, let's take a look at our traditional waterfall model that we have. So what we're going to do is we're going to begin the model by what a typical project manager does is they put together a project plan. And in that project plan, they set a series of milestones to say if they're on track or not. And let's say this is a large project with a large team, so what we'll find is we typically will have the first six seven eight months of the project as our analysis phase and we will be developing a whole series of documentation. This documentation will consist of things like our business requirements document, sometimes thousands of pages of business requirements. We'll have our what we call the logical design document, which will be business designs, designs of our business processes or what we might call our external processes and also our data model.

They'll look at the logical data model. Third, normal form fully attributes the data model. We'll have all of that created most times. We'll create a proposed architecture model as well, because if we understand what the requirements are, we will put together the documentation for the technical architecture proposal or proposed technical architecture, as well as a test strategy. This test lead will be put together based on the requirements of strategy for testing all of this. Well, that's going to take months and months of work. And what we do is we measure our progress based on how much documentation we have. So we'll say if we begin this project in January, the first milestone one is by the middle of February, February, we will have completed our business requirements document. We hit it.

We completed, we say we're on track, we're on time. So by the time we come to the end of the first six or seven months, we've got all this documentation and we say we're on time, but we only have one real deliverable and that deliverable is our working software. So we have not measured progress on what we are actually building, so when we get down to building the software, many times we end up with a problem. It's not what the customer wants. It's late. It's a lot of things that fall here. But in the agile world, we measure our progress based on how much working software we have created. We'll talk, we'll see all of that as we walk through the scrum framework. But I do want to emphasize this. I am not saying we do not have documentation. Please do not build a system without documentation.

We have lighter documentation. One of the key things and you won't find this in any scrum Book is scrum documentation. But one of the key things I've learned over the years is this: The only documentation you need from your system is you need documentation for the support team to support the software. You don't need all the design documentation. What we've typically done because we are siloed. We have all this design documentation because it's going to be handed off to another group in another location. They need everything written down. While in the agile world we're co-located. We sit together in the same room. We had a lot of conversations.

We call this collaboration that goes on. We don't need it all written down. We don't need to have all that documentation because it's not needed to support the software. So we'll talk more on that as we get down to that level during the scrum portion of the Book. So keep that in mind. We measure progress by the amount of working software that we have created. So that's it for this particular topic. And the agile principle number seven, and we will see you in agile principle number eight. Thank you.

Agile Principle 08

Welcome back to the studios of the online Agile Mastery Academy and welcome back to our Book scrum, the master class. We're currently in our chapter one, which is the agile overview, which is our foundation and we are chapter number four where we are looking at the 12 principles of agile that are upheld by the four values that we talked about earlier. And we're walking through each of the principals from a summarization level. We are in principle number eight now, which is topic seven since we covered two principles in one of our topics. So let's take a look at principle number eight. Principle number eight laid out in the Agile Manifesto says this. Agile processes promote sustainable development. The sponsors, developers and users should be able to maintain a constant pace indefinitely. Let's talk about that constant pace.

Our focus is on something that we call iterations. These are constrained periods of time, their fixed cycles of time and then scrum, we call these sprints. And what we do at the beginning of the project is we set specifically the time frame for a sprint. It does not change. I mentioned that in a minute, it is always fixed. And I always recommend this to teams. I have a Book on this, but the front end with my projects, which have always been successful, is that we lay out an agile project charter and don't get pushed back when people say, Well, that's a waterfall. No project charter is not a waterfall. We do it. PMA has laid it out for project managers. But what it is, it is a north star for your project. How can you run a project when you don't know the North Star? In other words, you don't know what you're navigating to. You don't have a vision.

You don't have a mission to achieve the vision. You don't have goals to achieve your mission, and you don't have objectives to achieve your goals. That's all laid out in the Agile Project Charter. And now. The edge of the scrum guide 2020 lays that out, that's needed, you need that up front and we'll talk about that when we go through the scrum guide. So we have this set at the beginning, fixed iterations. We go through those and these are anywhere from one to four weeks, one to four weeks. My typical projects I work with are two weeks. I would love to do one week, but many people struggle with that. We talked about that earlier on and they're always the same length in time. In other words, if you're doing two weeks, you always do two weeks, if you have a two week and then a one week, and you'll never be able to estimate, you'll never be able to plan, everything's going to fall apart on you.

And that is proof of it. And Jeff Sutherland, co-founders will say that very, very bluntly. So make sure that that's how you lay it out. So once you have that? Let me talk about this consistency, the ability to maintain the pace. Why? Why do we say you don't burn out? Well, I always like to liken this or use the metaphor of a long distance runner. I used to be a long distance runner. My brothers were marathon runners and I was a larger individual and I was a half marathon runner. But I would run marathons, training for half marathons, and one of the things we, as long distance runners, would always say is that we're looking for the rhythm. We want to find the rhythm. And what that means for a long distance runner is when your body hits a specific rhythm that it maintains and continues.

The body drops its consumption of oxygen, which means that you can run further. Your muscles are not building up as much lactic acid, which is tiring them and causing them to get sore as an agile team hits a rhythm. And that team, once it hits that rhythm, what will happen? It's happened 100 percent of the time for all the teams you will find, from sprint to sprint, productivity begins to increase. Jeff Sutherland talks about that. He said If you have the same team, I recommend you never break your teams down in the same team from project to project, he says. A new team on Project one, when you put that team on Project two, when they've completed Project one, will be at a minimum four times productivity than they were at the beginning of Team Project one. And that continues. So it's that constant pace. It's psychological. Let me explain it this way.

That may explain the rhythm, the cadence, as we like to call it this way. As we wrap up, let me explain this way. We as human beings have within us this inherent desire to see something completed. You're that way when you complete something, if you're doing a home renovation project, if you're doing a document, when you complete it, you feel good. You should feel good about it. And you're motivated to move on. If. What we're doing in our traditional waterfall process. He was producing a lot of documentation, but not our product, which is our software. Till later in the project, what you'll find is motivation begins to drop. You are not seeing that, you're not seeing your product, you're your software, you're not seeing it completed.

You're not seeing customers saying yes or no to it. All you're doing is producing documentation, but that's not your product. Your product is software. Sure, psychologically I tell project managers who back in the early days I trained, I would tell them this by the time you hit month three and four of your project read for motivation levels to dip, you begin to drop. That's when you need to keep people getting back on track. Why is it dropping? You're not seeing software developed. That's what they're for. So with all that said, that is the reason we talk about the fact that you need to have this specific time frame, but the cadence allows all the members just to keep working. They're motivated. It works. It works. So with that said, that's it for agile principle number eight. We will see you in agile principle number nine. Thank you.

Agile Principle 09

And welcome back to the studios of the Agile Mastery Academy and our Book scrum, the Master Class A game, we're going through the agile refresher portion of the Book we are in chapter four, which is looking at the 12 principles of agile. And in this particular topic for this chapter, we're dealing with agile principle number nine. I will not spend a lot of time on this principle since we dig deeply into it in our agile Book. Agile Part two. But what this principle nine states is this continuous attention. We give continuous attention again. We give continuous attention to technical excellence and good design. Why? Because this enhances agility. You can move and change quicker and faster when you have technical excellence.

So we're continually refactoring. We're continually focused on the excellence of we have a problem.We fix that problem. We don't leave it. Till the next release, you know, we call that technical debt as technical processes break or we plug things in. We're increasing the debt that we have, which we will never get rid of. So our focus is on excellence. This is something we have missed in our industry for the last 30 years or so as we have focused more on time to market as opposed to time to market with excellence. So agile is bringing excellence back in and a lot of this excellence aspect comes from the technical techniques we use.

We use a lot of these and these help us achieve excellence. We use things like test driven development. We use things like automated testing. These techniques allow us to achieve this excellence because they spot the problems quickly and they allow us not to have those problems. And we're focused on that. And when we do have them, we fix them. So that's what we're focused on in this particular topic and this particular principle that we're looking at excellence. So with that said, thank you very much. We will see you in the next principal agile principle number 10. Thank you.

Agile Principle 10

Welcome back to the studios of the online Agile Mastery Academy and welcome back to our core scrum, the master class. We're currently going to chapter one, which is our agile overview and chapter number four, where we've broken down each of our 12 principles of agile which is upheld by the four values. This is all part of our agile manifesto. It's part of our foundation, which scrum is built upon. So in this particular topic, this chapter, we're in topic number nine and we're looking at agile principles. 10. I really like this principle. I like them all, but this is one I really like and this is what it states, which is really interesting. It says this. It says agile is about simplicity, and an agile simplicity is essential. It's essential.

And what is simplicity is the art of maximizing the amount of work not done. We say that again, it's the art of maximizing the amount of work not done. Not done, not maximizing the amount of work we do is maximizing the amount of work not done well, what do we mean by that? Well, what we're saying and I've talked about this and I really dig deep in our agile, our agile Book. What is real agile? I talk about the fact that what you're finding is we have on an ongoing basis within our organization changes taking place all around the organization, changes taking place in business rules and in government, in our economic system and customers in the business size itself and business personnel. All of these changes are continually happening as we're building the system.

So what we're going to do is we're going to ensure that as those changes are appearing, we are adjusting our Book. We're taking things out. For example, we have a product backlog. We're taking things out of that product backlog because we no longer need them. What we want to focus on is exactly what the company needs when we deliver that software. So here's a set of statistics that have been around for a few years. They have actually increased, but we're using the older ones because they're not as out of their way out there. But this is what we have. We have a picture that says in a typical traditional system, the waterfall system, what we develop in that system, 45 percent of the functionality we deliver is never used. 45 never used 19 percent is very rarely used, which equates to, as it says, in the lower left of that chapter, 64 percent of what we build into a traditional system is never or rarely used, and I've done a lot of audits of systems over the years and I get this from the clients. Yes, we probably will not use a lot of it. So our focus in Agile is not to put all of that in there, remember I talked about in the traditional way of operating, we capture all the requirements for thousands of pages of requirements. Why, as we travel through building that system, many of those requirements disappear because they're no longer needed or they have to be modified. So that is that big blue chapter there. But if we're doing it the traditional way, we deliver that two years, three years later, we deliver that set of requirements from three years ago when the business isn't there any longer.

So 64 percent is derived from that. So what we focus on as an agile is top business value and priority, which is that seven percent always. Thirteen percent often and sometimes we always deliver that and we'll deliver partway into the purple. But our focus is on maximizing the amount of work we don't do because we don't want to deliver unused work work that will never be used. So keep that in mind. That is our focus that maximizes the amount of work we don't do. That is principle number 10 straight from the Agile Manifesto. So thank you very much for sitting through this chapter. This topic, we will see you in agile principle number one two from the end. Thank you.

Agile Principle 11

Welcome back to the studios of the online Agile Mastery Academy and welcome back to our core scrum, the master class. We're currently going through what we call chapter one of our Book, which is the agile refresher, and we're looking at the fourth chapter, which is dealing with the 12 principles of agile. You need to understand these. You need to understand how they fit into scrum, which is what this Book is about. This is your foundation. If you don't have the foundation, scrum will fail. So we're dealing with these and we are now currently on topic number 10, which is agile principles 11. The one from the end, we're almost done with these particular principles that we're focused on. So let's look at principle number 11.

Principle number 11 says this. The best architectures, the best requirements, the best designs emerge from self-organizing teams, that word emerge is important here because what it indicates is that things are not set in stone, they are evolving. And I always say this, we don't create systems in the agile world. Our systems emerge. They're an emergency. System that we're building, it's a product that emerges, so let's talk about this, let's talk about the teams, we talk about the facts. Yet these emerging systems, we need self-organizing teams. So let's look at an eight scrum team, and I'm going to lay out four criteria for a scrum team. First of all, they're small to eight people. Well, what about a large project, you say? Well, we have multiple small teams. Small teams are critical from a communication perspective, and we'll talk about that in our teams Book.

We'll talk about how we are cognitively limited as human beings in capturing lines of communication. And we know that over eight people on the team, things become dropped or they drop out. Things become gray in the communication process. So we keep our teams small. It's a psychological thing. They're cross-functional. In other words, we don't have a small team of business analysts and a small team of developers and a small team of testers know every function that's needed to turn that software out is on each team. In other words, we have business analysts, we have business archerd architects, we'll have data architects, we'll have developers and testers all required to deliver that piece of software that we're working on.

So they're cross-functional. All those functions are within the team, and you hear the term cross-functional. Often that's what we mean, and they self-organize. So on a daily basis, for example, I'll give you what one of the things that I've encountered many times is a team does its daily scrum. And as we're talking to the daily scrum, we notice we have some impediments which are brought up. We put those in the parking lot and so we don't consume more than 15 minutes. We then after the meeting, we then take our time to discuss these impediments. And what will happen many times is you have things like, for example, the tester may say, you know, we didn't plan for this much testing and there's no way we can get this done in two days and we have a review of our software with our stakeholders by the end of tomorrow.

It won't be done. So what the team does is they say, OK, two of the members say, Well, you know, I'm ahead of my schedule. What I'm going to do is I will help you. Let's take a look at what we can do. And they will swarm on that. And instead of taking two days, they'll get it out of the way in two hours and they're back on track. So they self-organize based on the need of the day, the need of the week, the need of the month, there's self-organization that goes on. I will say this many times in this Book that in the scrum, we are not role focused. We are goal focused. We do whatever it takes. You have an ice hockey team.

You have specific roles, but those roles will change based on what happens. For example, a defenseman gets hold of a breakaway on a puck. They're not just going to drop back while I'm a defenseman. No, they're going to go for the net and shoot that they become. They become a center. They self-organize. And one at one of the one of the one of the people from the front line would drop back and defend the goal while that defenseman is taking the puck down. So they are self-organizing and we do that in our scrum development, product development teams and finally, teams are autonomous.

They make the decisions and that discussion, they make the decisions. Well, what about the scrum masters grandmasters there to facilitate this? Scrum Master is in every meeting reading. They have immense responsibility and we'll talk about that as we get into the rules of Scrum. So that is our principle number 11. So we're focused on teams and we'll talk a lot more on that. Principle number 11 from The Agile Manifesto. So thank you very much, and we will see you in our next chapter on the next topic, which will be agile. Principle 12 the final of the 12 Principles. Thank you.

Agile Principle 12

Welcome back to the studios of the online Agile Mastery Academy and welcome back to our core scrum, the master class. And in this particular chapter, which we're going to be continuing with, is our agile review or agile overview or agile refresher. I really want to say it's all based on what has come out of our first two Books. Agile, the real agile part one and part two. And we just want to make sure that you have that foundation. So we are in chapter four of that. And chapter four is the focus on the 12 principles of agile. These are the 12 principles that come from our agile manifesto. This is what we base our foundation on. In scrum, it is essential that we understand and know this for our foundation.

So what we've done is we've taken those and broken them into topics. One of our topics, we had two actual principles, so that's why we are topic 11 final topic that we're going to be looking at. And this is chapter four. And this is our final chapter that we're looking at in this chapter and we're looking at agile principle number 12, the final principle that we work with in the agile world. And Principle 12 says this. It's laid out at regular intervals. The team reflects on how to become more effective and then tunes and adjusts its behavior accordingly. So here's how I like to lay it out. We're focused on continuous improvement.

The first 11 principles that we've looked at are focused on continually improving the product we're building. We're continually improving that well. This one is looking at continually improving our process or how we're building that product. So again, keep this in mind. The first 11 agile principles focus on improving the product. The 12th one focuses on improving our process of building the product. So we're looking at how we're doing it, and I always like to say that you're going to find within an organization that over time, no two teams will be identical. They're all fitting into the environment they're working with.

They're adapting to their environment, the people, the processes, the area of the business, the geographic location. And that's going to change from team to team, from project to project. So you're going to be seeing that as they go through a retrospective. They're going to adapt to what they're doing and how they're doing it. So this is a critical thing that we look at. We're always looking at improving and we do that by asking three questions. During our retrospective, first of all, I focus on this. I focus and we'll talk about this in the ceremony, looking at what went well in the last iteration because we want to replicate that once we've talked to that and then we'll talk about the challenges we had.

What were the challenges? What were the challenges with people? What were the challenges with their process? What were the challenges with working together? And then what we'll do is we'll put together action items that we're going to take to fix those challenges. And that will be and we're looking at an example. I use a Trello board with my teams and that's the third call and these are the action items. And then when we begin the next retrospective at the end of the next sprint, the first thing we talk about are those action items. Did we achieve what we wanted to achieve? If we did, would they become action items again? So we're focused continually on improving, but not just laying out what our challenges are and what our challenges were, but actually putting together action items, assigning those items for the next sprint.

That's the job of the scrum master to coordinate that, to make sure that it's done. So that's it, that's it for the 12 principles of the Agile Manifesto. These are again, the 12 principles that scrum is based on. Everything we do in Scrum has to fit this. If somebody comes to you and says, Well, you know, in scrum, this is a great thing to do, but we want to do this, and I think that's great. But you show me what principle, what value does that address in the value pillars? And then what principles are the foundation to what you're talking about doing? If it's not there, I won't do it. I want to ensure that everything we do in scrum adheres to the values and the principles of the Agile Manifesto. That's why they're there. So thank you very much. So we've come to the end of the fourth chapter.

The fourth chapter was dealing with the 12 principles of the Agile Manifesto. We broke those down into topics. We did each topic separately, so we've come to the end of the Prince 12 principle chapter. So go back. Review these. Make sure you have an understanding of them. If you've got some questions, do some research. Everything is online. Go over to Scrum Dot or go check out their blogs. Check out the frequently asked questions. Check out the discussion list. You get all your answers there. So this is the foundation that we're setting for a scrum. So that's it for chapter number four, which is the principles of the Agile Manifesto, and we will see you in our next chapter. Thank you.

Why We Use Agile Part 1

And welcome back to the studios of the online ad show Mastery Academy, and welcome back to our Book scrum master class. What we're doing is we're currently moving through chapter one, which is our agile overview or agile refresher, and we're beginning a new less and less and number six. And in this chapter, we're looking at why we use agile. Why is this something that we would use on our products projects? What does it do for us, so let's take a look at it. Agile gives us the ability to adapt as we're building a product to be able to, as I like to say, turn on a dime. If we're heading in a direction that is shown to be wrong, we have the ability to instantly turn from that direction to a new direction. We call it turning on a dime.

It's not like that super oil tanker that takes so much resources just to do a shift in direction. We want to be able to move very quickly, and we want to be able to change direction continually. So this isn't just a one time thing. We want to be able to do this on a continual basis because our environment around us is changing and we'll see that in this chapter. And we also want the ability to stop a project, regroup quickly and then take a new attack on that project when things aren't working. And that happens with many of our products that we're building and we need to take a stop and quickly regroup while agile allows us to do that, and then we can adjust our Book quickly. We can quickly change Book and we can change.

Many Books will look at that again. So agile allows us to do that as we're building a product or as we're working on our project, as we like to say. So is this necessary to do, is it necessary to actually be able to do all of this really, really well? Forrester made this comment. No, Forrester's one of our oversight organizations, and they made this comment a few years ago, way back in 2012 January as we began that year. And I remember when this document came out, it was kind of a little bit shaky, too many I.T. information groups and they said this. The organizational structures that got us to 2012 are failing us. They are not the structures that will take us forward. So the way we had worked in building products in the IT industry, they said this is not going to work anymore. What we've done is failing.

Times have changed and our organizations must adapt to catch up and begin to keep pace with business change. This is the biggest thing we're dealing with. We're dealing with business change and that is happening faster and faster and faster. We call it the volatility of our business world. So Forrester made that statement back in 2012. They said what got us to this point in time won't work any further on. And many companies today are still using those same structures, and it's failing them. So agile is what we're using to change that we're adapting and agile is a way we do it. So how do we do this? How do we do this? Well, we like to say that our focus is on using an agile product development philosophy.

We're looking at building products and it doesn't just have to be information technology, but we use this a lot in information technology. I've trained groups in policy generation, in the government arenas. They have nothing to do with it as policy and it has been a tremendous improvement to what they're doing from a policy development process. We see it in organizational design. How do we change an organization, redesign it? Agile is the perfect way to do this or company start ups. Jeff Sutherland, our co-founder of Scrum, has spent a number of years working with technical technology startups and using scrum to do it, and it's very successful. So there are many, many different types of products, and we see automobile manufacturing works well, scrum works well in that arena.

We see this with a vehicle developed by a small company out of Seattle, Washington. It's actually a global company because it includes people from many countries. And you can look up wiki speed, and they've developed a road legal car that in the U.S. gets more than 100 miles to a gallon of gasoline. And they've used scrum to do this, and they're continually revamping and changing. So product development. Agile is the way to develop products using the agile approach. Your standard information technology way, which is standard in many product developments, is we're shooting for a target and we're shooting for a fixed target. But that's not how our industry works. That's not how the world around us works, I should say not our industry, but the world. The target is not fixed.

It's moving. So what we've attempted to do in moving towards a fixed target is to use a linear process. You know, people say waterfall, it's a cycle. No, it's not. It's linear. The waterfall process only goes in one direction. Waterfall only goes down. You don't find water going back up the waterfall. Same with our waterfall development. Once we get moving, it's almost impossible to go back. And what do I mean by that? Well, let's take a look and an I.T. information technology development process. We've got our QE and our project management spreading out throughout the project. But how we set it up is this way we have a definition phase. We define what we're going to work on. We do our cause and effect analysis. We understand the pain points and we put together a business case which we present might take three to four months.

I know some organizations take at least a year to do a business case once we've done that. We have got approvals and we're now doing our analysis and we do our own. We've talked about our business requirements. Reports are logical designs. Our technical architecture targets our test strategies. And then when we come to the end and everybody agrees to it, we then move on to our physical design. We do all our physical, our UI designs, our database, a detailed database, physical designs, generating schemas, testing all of that. And then we go into our construction. We're finally building our software.

And you see, this is moving down and then we get into testing and finally, we should be implementing. But what typically happens is we get into our testing and we find out this isn't what the customer wants. So we need to go back to analysis and start finding out changing our requirements, changing our design. That's a horrendous process. It takes a ton of time and we never achieve our initial goals. We can't go back out. So what our focus is is that we understand the target that we're shooting for is moving because we are no longer at the beginning where a business was when we started. Things have changed.

Our target has moved, so we need to focus on a moving target, not a fixed target. So keep that in mind. Fixed target versus a moving target. So that's as far as we're going to go with this portion of the chapter, they've got a bit more time in there and I don't want to get too much time in these chapters. So we're going to take a chapter break now, go back through that and understand why we use agile. Listen to that again. And then once you've done that, move on to our next chapter and we'll see you there. Thank you.

Why We Use Agile Part 2

Welcome back to the studios of the online Agile Mastery Academy and our Book scrum, the master class currently in chapter one of the Book and in chapter one, we're doing an agile overview or an agile refresher however you want to look at it, and we are in chapter six, which is looking at why we use agile and we're in part two of chapter six. So we've talked about in part one, we've talked about the fact that we have traditionally been focused on a fixed target by using our linear waterfall approach. And the problem we have is that it does not address what we're really facing, which is a moving target. And so when we get to the spot where the target is supposed to be at the end of the project, it's no longer there.

And I want to kind of back that up with this. These thoughts from Steve McConnell Steve McConnell runs an organization, a consulting firm in Seattle, Washington, doing a lot of work with Microsoft called Constructs. And Steve is an author of many books and one of his earlier books Code Complete and then Code Complete two. He gave us a picture, and in that picture he showed us and told us about this thing that he called the cone of uncertainty. And most of us at that time fully agreed. Most of us in the senior executive region of I.T. agreed with him. And from this graphic, you can see that what we face at the beginning of any project is this massive amount of uncertainty.

And as we go through our requirements analysis exercise, we still have much, much uncertainty even into our detailed design and into construction. And what we typically do when we face uncertainty is we make assumptions, business makes assumptions, it makes assumptions. And one of the things we see in the agile world, I may sound a little rough, but. The assumption is the mother of all screw ups. That's where our mistakes happen in the agile world if we make assumptions. So what we focus on are the things that we know and those things that are uncertain slowly emerge with certainty. You know, it's interesting that the group that oversees the International Business Analysis Arena, the IPA, made a comment about five years ago, and they said, we have determined something.

We have determined that there is something in our development, in the software arena, in the development process that we call the emergent requirement. These are requirements that you would never know at the beginning of a project, at the beginning of a system, at the beginning of a development, but they emerge as things begin to appear. Well, with the way we've traditionally done our projects, we can't fit those in and that's been the problem now. Steve said that he had a webinar in I believe it was 2015, and I sat in on that webinar and he said, I have good news and bad news. People, we no longer face a cone of uncertainty. Wow, that's good news.

But what we face is a cloud of uncertainty, a massive amount of uncertainty right to the end of any project. And we'll talk about that in a minute. Why is there? Uncertainty will show you why there's uncertainty. But what he was saying is that you will never get to the point where you've got everything nailed down. You will have to take what you know. Build on that and what you know, will take some of that uncertainty in the future. Out of the way, you will be able to work on that and slowly what the business needs will emerge from it. So I'm going to give you this little picture that I'd like to draw for my students, both in academia and in the corporate world of the difference between our traditional waterfall way of working in agile and how we see agile working and why it works.

So let's take a look at it. So here we are. We're going to do a scenario here where we are back on October 1st of 2018, and we are putting together a business case for an ERP for our organization, a financial ERP. And we work at that. We put together all the high level requirements and we put together our risks that we're facing, our business risks and our project risks. And we come up with a high level estimate, high level estimate. We understand what the pain points are for the organization and what we have to eliminate and what we do in that business case as we put together a timeline. And on January 1st, 2019, we got it all approved. And what it tells us is that by December the 31st 2020, we will have hit a target. We've set the target, that's what we're shooting for.

So we begin the process. We go through our analysis phase and we put together documents like the Requirements Report and the logical models and the Target Architecture Report, our test strategy and by October the 1st 2019. Seven months later, we got it signed off. We finally get everybody to agree to it or those who we need, and now we begin working on our physical design of that logical design. We put together our UI prototypes, our data structure models, our application architecture models, and by December the 1st 2019, we've completed all that documentation and we get it signed off and we say we're on track. We're meeting our milestones now we begin construction. It might be pure custom development within our organization.

It might be software as a service, renting in the cloud, a portion of it in the cloud. We might be doing some cots commercial off the shelf software we'd purchase licensing. I love going on a lot of configuration, going on a lot of programming going on, and what happens is by our timeframe, we've got our unit test cases, we've got our integration testing, we've got our system testing. And by October, the 1st 2020, three months away from our target, we get it all agreed to. And now we begin testing, we go to our final U80 user acceptance testing. And what happens is the businesses know. That's not what we need now. You see, the target is no longer there.

The target is down here. It has shifted and we've been moving towards the wrong spot. So we go back hat in hand to the business and ask for more money and millions of dollars and more time. And so they give us six months reluctantly and more money. And we set our new target for June the 1st 2021, and we begin working towards it. And when we get there, it's no. Our clients say that's not what we need. Now you see the targets no longer there. So that has been the problem that we've been trying to deal with. And the question is why is that happening? Well, you see the business case that we had was done as of January the 1st. It was signed off that our requirements were all based on where we were at that point in time.

Now, there's only one way that you can put together a requirements document that will meet the needs of the business when you deliver, and that is if you have a crystal ball and no one has found one yet, you cannot predict the future. So what happens is, as we're moving along this line, we're two months into it or one month into it and the world changes. We have some economic disasters and then the world changes again. We have a new government, new rules again, the world changes and all of this is impacting our financial system. We have a new business that we've purchased. Our organization has spread out. We've got new products, we've got a lot of new things that we're dealing with. Our executive now has changed.

We've got a new executive all the way along this line that we're working on this product that we signed off on January the 1st 2019. Our world is changing. So no wonder we're not meeting the needs of the business, so what does Agile do? Well, it's October the 1st 2018. We put together something that we call an agile business case and it won't get into it. Now I have a Book on the agile business case. And from that? We get approvals and we set a target. No, we don't say that. We don't know where we're going, we knew we were going. But as we begin the summer, the first we begin writing software, we're not waiting till December or January, the 1st or December the 1st 2019, we're writing software December 2018 and we're doing this in these increments or the sprints, and we begin working based on enough information.

We don't have all the requirements, we can't have all the requirements. We've talked about that it's impossible to know where the future is going to be, but we know what is high priority and what we do know now what is certain, and we work on that certainty and we're partway through it where let's see, we're a month, two months into it and we find out from our clients through our feedback loop that know what we're developing. It's not actually going to meet the need today. So what do we do? We shift our trajectory. We set a new target and we shift and we're going to move towards that target where the business thinks they'll be.

And we start moving down that trajectory and then we get the word as they see what we're doing that, no, it's not actually going to meet our needs. These things have changed, so we shift the trajectory again. Our target has shifted and we begin moving down every sprint. We have feedback. We have feedback. Now these time frames are too large, but I'm just giving you a pictorial perspective. And again, we get the message from our business. No, that's not where the target is going to be. We've got some new things that have come in and now it has shifted and we shift with it. And we keep moving down and suddenly we get the same message. It's shifted again and we hit it exactly where the business is.

When we deliver that software, exactly what they need, when we deliver the software, does it work? It works. It has worked 100 percent of the time for me for 20 years now. So yes, that is how the agile world works. But you have to do it right. You have to have an understanding. The business has to have an understanding, the senior executive has to have an understanding, and I can't stress that enough. They have to have an understanding of what is going on. Otherwise, it won't work. I'll be blunt, I have been called into too many companies, and I've had to say I'm sorry, but without your executive knowing what you're doing, you cannot do it. They're expecting something totally different and they're asking for something totally different.

So that's what we look at, the difference between our traditional way of developing and our original way of developing, and we get the big check mark the thumbs up. This is what we need. So that covers what I wanted to cover in this chapter when I talk about why agile and how we're using agile, this is what I wanted to talk through here. So go back and review, especially this chapter. Go back and review it and make sure you understand what I am saying when I talk about this cone of uncertainty and how we deal with that uncertainty from an agile perspective and using scrum. So go back to review it and we will see you in our next chapter. Thank you.

Agile Frameworks

Welcome back to the studios of the online Agile Mastery Academy and welcome back to our core scrum, the masterclass. We are in our agile review chapter or our agile refresher chapter, chapter one, and we are in less than seven and less than seven. We're going to talk about agile frameworks. This is where we wrap up the agile refresher portion and move into scrum. But I want to talk about these things that we call frameworks, the agile frameworks. These are how we apply the 12 principles within our projects that we're working on, as I say here, we apply the 12 principles with one or more of the agile frameworks. So the question is what do you mean by framework versus a methodology? Well, our methodology, as I've mentioned before, is a prescribed way of addressing the development of a product. We've laid out a list of things that have to be done.

We call it a checklist. And as we go through, we check each thing off. We've done this, we've done this, we've done this. And when we come to the end, we should have a successful product. But we cannot prescribe how to build, for example, a software product. It doesn't work, and that's the problem we face because each development is different. Each product development is different. And let me explain that in a way, the metaphor I draw here when I explain a framework is I draw a metaphor that a framework is essentially a pattern. You have a pattern of how you're going to work with this product. But within the pattern, you have many different ways of dealing with it.

Let me give you a metaphorical example. Here I am an individual who in the corporate arena and in teaching in the university environment, I wear a suit and tie and my signature snakeskin western cowboy boots. That's just who I am now. My suits are tailor made. Some are tailor made in Korea. In Seoul. Some are made in Shanghai. I travel sometimes to get the main. There are. Some are made here at home. Now all the suits have the same pattern and they have for the years that I've been doing this since the 70s, they all have a pair of slacks with two legs and a jacket with two arms. Now that's the pattern. But within the pattern, I can have many, many different ways of operating a kind of a short jacket that can have a long jacket. I can have one button to button, three buttons, four buttons.

I can have wide lapels, narrow lapels. I can have pockets, no pockets, pockets with flaps. I can have an event in the back. I can have a double event in the back. I can have no vents in the back. The slacks, I can have high waisted, mid waisted, low waisted. I can have square pockets, straight pockets, slanted pockets, no pockets. I can have narrow pants, short, long, wide. Back in the 70s, I would have 30 36 inch wide bottoms on my pants and my slacks. I can have cuffs or no cuffs, so the pattern is always the same. But how we work within the pattern differs in my case from a fashion perspective. But in the business world, it's going to differ based on your environment, the people you're working with, the business you're working with, the area of the business, you're working with the business rules and it goes on and on and on.

So we have frameworks that we use, and I'm going to break down some of these frameworks for you to give you a categorization that I like to use and many of us use. We talk about the fact that there are three types of frameworks. We have a planning framework. I'll give you one planning framework disciplined, agile from Scott Ambler. It's not only a single project framework, it is what we call a skilled, agile framework. Scott Ambler and Mark live. This is their product. They've sold it to PMI a year and a half ago from the time I'm doing this chapter.

So the Project Management Institute now has it as their framework of choice when you're learning to be an agile project manager. Then we have our software engineering frameworks, the one most people know about extreme programming created by who we call the three extremes can't back Ward Cunningham and Ron Jeffries or uninvite Ron and I. I have had so many conversations online. Then we have feature driven development. Jeff DeLuca at the Bank of Singapore in the early 2000s replaced an entire ERP and one year very successfully using the feature driven development. We have Crystal from Alistair Cochranc. You've been in the agile world.

You've heard the term visible information radiators that comes from Alistair Cockburn. We have Jim Highsmith, who he talked about a little while ago as one of the signers of The Agile Manifesto. He's about the end of APM, the agile, agile project management. These are just some of the frameworks out there. Then we are at some of the software engineering frameworks there, and we have the system DSM, the SDM, the dynamic systems development method as well. Just these are, I'd say, five of the 13 that we have or 13 or 14 that I'm aware of. And then we have the agile management frameworks.

There are two, there is scrum Jeff Sutherland, Ken Schwager, co-founders. And then we have Kanban, we have Dave Anderson from Florida and Mr Callaway.

Alan Shallowly from Seattle, Washington. Really big behind Kanban and lean. So these are the two agile management frameworks where we borrow techniques from the other software engineering frameworks. Repackage them in these frameworks. So I'll talk about Scrum. That's where we're going to go. Our focus is on scrum and this is one of the statistical perspectives of the usage of scrum globally that we have from a couple of years ago now. It's increased since then, but at that point fifty four percent of shops worldwide were pure scrum shops and another 10 percent were scrum and extreme high extreme programming hybrids. So here we have 64 percent of organizations using scrum to some form and then another eight percent of scrum band kind of a combination between Scrum and Kanban, and I teach that as well.

So here we have over 70 percent of organizations globally using scrum to some degree, 74 to 80 percent of organizations. So that's why we focus on it. It is the framework of choice for many organizations in their product development, lots in the I.T. world, information technology, world, software development and hardware implementation. But many other types of organizations are using it now. So this is what we have available to us. So that ends this chapter that we're talking about from an agile perspective. chapter one and it ends our chapter seven, which is on agile framework. So here we come. We come to the end of agile refresher and the end of our agile frameworks chapter, and we move into scrum now pure scrum. So with that said, thank you. Go back through this to understand your frameworks and what a framework is very, very important and we will see you in our next chapter. Thank you.

Introduction To Scrum

Welcome back to the studios of the online Agile Mastery Academy. And welcome back to our Book scrum master class. We are now beginning chapter two of the Book chapter so I've just labeled it scrum. We're going to spend a fair bit of time in this chapter learning about this framework that we call scrum. So this is chapter one of scrum and in chapter one of the chapter, we're going to talk about an introduction. I want you to understand where this came from. This is going to give you some good insight as you work with scrum in your organizations when you think about where it came from and how it started. So let's go back and talk about agile. You say, Well, wait a minute, we're talking. Scrum. Yes, Scrum is based on agile, so we want to talk about how scrum came from here.

So again, I'm going to emphasize, as I have in the past chapters, that agile is not about software. It was not first created for software development. It was not first used in software development. It is not a software methodology that you hear so many people talking about. But it came from two Japanese professors, Mr Takeuchi and Mr Know. And they wrote a paper in the 1986 Harvard Business Review, which turned the manufacturing product development world on its ear. And it was quite interesting in that document, there's a few over the Book of my chapters. You'll hear a few of the excerpts from that document, but they're not big excerpts. These small little nuggets cause people to think.

Maybe there is a different way to do this, and in the Harvard Business Review, this particular paragraph really shook up. A lot of people made them think they said this. The relay race approach to product development. Straight out of the Harvard Business Review, so in our product development, if you're looking in the information technology world, what do we do? The business analyst comes along and puts together all the upfront, high level business requirements, the business case. And then once it's approved, they turn it over to the systems analyst. The systems analyst does their part and then they hand the baton off to the applications architect who does their part, and they hand the baton off to the dev leads who do their part, and they hand off the baton to the programmers and the configuration experts who do their part.

They hand the baton off to the testers and they do their part and then hand the baton off to the implementation coordinators. The relay race approach where they said this may conflict with the goals of maximum speed and flexibility, which it absolutely does. An interesting metaphor they use instead is a holistic or rugby approach where a team tries to go the distance as a unit, passing the ball back and forth. This may better serve today's competitive requirements, so in their words, that individual running and handing the baton off to the next individual does not work or probably does not work.

They were very gentle in their words, but we know it does not work. So why not use a team approach, which is what came out of this whole philosophy? So what's really interesting is that within a year, Toyota hired both of these professors who came on board and out of their involvement with Toyota came the Toyota production system, the TPS, which is still known as the number one automobile manufacturing system in the world. There's a lot of things to say about it, but this is where it came from. From that article written in the Harvard Business Review. So here's where it's being used. Is being used as a product in automobile development. Well, what happened is in information technology in that arena.

In 1993, at the Esso Corporation, a gentleman by the name of Jess Sutherland, an ex fighter pilot from the Vietnam War, earned many doctorate degrees in high level cancer research, working with banks straightening them out. in 1993 at Esso Corporation was working with a team of 300 to put together a fourth generation programming language. And what he did is he brought in a new way of doing it. And it was called scrum and he brought in a gentleman by the name of Ken Shaver. So Jeff Sutherland and Ken Shaver are known as the co-authors of Scrum. Jeff runs Scrum Inc and can scrum board where we get our. Scrum guide for them, but they partnered together again, they're very much together in all of this.

The scrum is a very simple framework. This is a picture of it. We begin with a product backlog which uses a sprint backlog. We go through a one two three four week sprint and we deliver working Rene's software. And that sounds really simple and easy. That's all we do. But it's how we do it, and it's what takes place between our ears to get it done and to do it right that causes us the most consternation. So we want to talk about that. So this is scrum. This is the process that we have. So in 1995, at an object oriented programming conference, a global conference in Texas, Ken and Jeff presented this two years later after they had started. They presented this and it took the conference by storm. People were excited to hear of the results that they had achieved through using this framework that they called Scrum.

And essentially, what they explained was the fact that this was a framework that was all about change based on the environment that you're working in and you're continually changing based on the changes in the environment. And I love this metaphor that actually comes from our two Japanese professors about rugby. But I like to explain this way. I have played a number of years of American football, and we were playing in the same conditions. We would have our goal for the game or vision for the game. And that did not vary. What varied is how we achieved it, if we were. If you look on the right, a left hand picture of when we played on a sunny grassy field we played on. We had the same goal as when we played on the other picture on a rainy, muddy day on a muddy field.

We had the same goal and vision, but we played it entirely differently. Our vision was to win the game. But we achieved it. We achieved it differently, and that's what we're talking about with scrum. Scrum is a framework that we're going to adapt. And bring in change into our project based on what's happening with the environment as we're working through it. So that's kind of an overview of the beginning of it, and we'll talk a little more about what the next steps were. And as we get into that, we're going to start to learn about Scrum. So thank you very much. We will take a break here and then we will move into our next chapter so you can go back and listen to this and then be prepared to start learning about Scrum. Thank you.

The Scrum Guide

And welcome back to the studios of the online Agile Mastery Academy and welcome back to our core scrum, the master class. So we've talked through the whole foundational aspect of Scrum, which is the agile philosophy, and we're in chapter two now, which is our chapter on scrum. And what I want to talk about in this chapter is something that we called the scrum guide, which we will be referring to and viewing throughout the entire Book. So I want to give you an introduction to it and to give you that introduction, I'm going to tell you about the two authors. Author number one is Jeff Sutherland, who is chairman of Scrum Inc.

Again, as I mentioned earlier, Jeff is a fighter pilot veteran who came back into the workforce as a university professor and then into research, working on cancer research and then moving into working with banks, pulling them out of problems. And then we talked about it as a consultant with an easel corp and everything just exploded from there. So he's chairman of Scrum Inc and as well, his partner, the Copart co-founder, is chairman of Scrum Talk, and that's Ken Schwarber. And we will hear from Ken as well during the Book. So these are the two gentlemen who partnered together and they partner putting together the scrum guide now who has been brought on board. And I bring this up for a particular reason is Jeff Sutherland Jr. JJ.

As he is known, he is now the CEO of the corporation. And he wrote this quote two years ago, and it's something that I think really says a lot. In a few words, this is the quote. In December of 1993, my father, Jeff Sutherland, gathered a team of people and asked them to go on a new journey with him, a new way of working, the way he had started developing 40 years prior. While a cadet at West Point developed through years as a fighter pilot, as a professor seeking new treatments for cancer and leading six different technology companies. Now this is what I've highlighted: a way of working rooted in respect for people, a way to unleash human potential, a way that delivers results faster than anyone had ever thought possible, a way with the unlikely name of scrum.

And to me, that sums it all up. That is what we're working with, and it is very exciting. It's an exciting way to work. So this is the foundation from a people perspective, and I always like to go back and talk about the foundation. Foundation is required for anything to remain to stand and scrum will not stand without the foundation. We have two foundations that we talk about here. Foundation number one is our agile philosophy, which we have talks through the agile philosophy and the other part of our foundation is the scrum guide. So this is what I want to introduce in this chapter, and I want to introduce it by reading just a couple of paragraphs from the November 2020 scrum guide. So this was put up.

This is the latest one. I am recording this as of August 2021, so it hasn't even been a year yet, and I was in on a conference three, actually a three day conference webinar that they had in regards to explaining all the nuances and aspects of the scrum guide. So this is what I want to read from the guide, and this is what it says. The scrum guide contains the definition of scrum.

Each element of the framework serves a specific purpose that is essential to the overall value and results realized from scrum. Changing the core design or ideas of scrum, leaving out elements or not following the rules of scrum covers up problems and limits the benefits of scrum, potentially even rendering it useless.

And I've seen this happen. Oh yes, we know ways to change it and we can change it. Yeah, it has rendered useless and they have not achieved any success. Scrum is simple. Try it as is and determine if his philosophy, theory and structure help to achieve goals and create value. The scrum listens to this. This is major. The scrum framework is purposefully incomplete. Is purposefully incomplete, and I will draw on that as I teach the Book. They have purposefully not set it up as an all encompassing methodology. It is incomplete because it has to fit into your organization. Only defining the parts required to implement scrum theory.

Scrum is built upon by the collective intelligence of the people using it, rather than provide people with detailed instructions. The rules of scrum guide their relationships and interactions. Interesting statement relationships and interactions. It tells us something about scrum. It's about people. The fundamental unit of Scrum is a small team of people. A scrum team. The scrum team consists of one scrum master, one scrum master. I emphasize that because I have to deal with organizations that have teams that have scrum master's or even three. One scrum master, one product owner and developers. That's the team. Within a scrum team, there are no sub teams or hierarchies. It is a cohesive unit of professionals focused on one objective at a time. The product goal. That's what we have in our agile project charter. The product goal.

Only as an introduction, successful use of scrum depends on people becoming more proficient in living the five scrum values. And that's where we're going to go in our next chapter, we're going to talk about the five scrum values. And again, that's part of our foundation, so you need to know all of this before you understand the process. And that's why I emphasize this up front. And if you're going for someone, you need to know all of this. You're going to get questions in regards to all of this. In attempting to get your certification. So go back through this again. Listen to what I have read. You'll find that I have a scrum guide as one of the resources for the Book. You'll have access to download the scrum guide to go through it. Go through what I've done here. Don't have a scrum guide yet. Take the portions as I talked to them. It's easier for you to learn that way. So that is it. For this particular chapter, we're going to take a break in this chapter, scrum chapter two and we will move on to our next chapter and we will see you there. Thank you.

The Scrum Values

Welcome back to the studios of the online ad John Mastery Academy, and welcome back to our Book scrum master class. So we're moving through our scrum chapter now and we're in chapter number two and in chapter number two. What we're going to talk through are the scrum values, and you will find these in the scrum guide. I'm not going to read them from the guide, but I'm going to explain them to you. And from a perspective of values, these are the things that the scrum team values. So we have a lot of individuals, but these are not individual values, they are individual values from the perspective that they are a community of values. These are what the scrum teams value. These are the things that are valued, the five most important things valued by the scrum team.

And this does not vary. This is what scrum masters work to have achieved on their team. They're responsible for ensuring the team understands the values, owns the values, works with the values and loves the values. So let's talk about the five values. The first one is commitment. And let's look at a definition from Merriam Webster's dictionary. Commitment is an agreement or pledge to do something in the future. So our teams commit to doing the product and having it ready in the future. And we talk about the commitment achieved on the team by having these scrum teams work together as a unit, the team must not work as a group of separate individuals, but it is a unit that is collaborating and working together. That's why we encourage teams that are in a local location to be in a co-located structure, working in one room, working together, working as a unit.

And that's a critical word here. It takes a while before a team becomes a unit, and that's the responsibility of the scrum master. We talk about that in our scrum master Book. We have a Book specifically on the scrum master and we deal with how they do that. What is their responsibility? Team members trust each other big word here, and you won't find that on a new team initially, it is up to the scrum master to ensure that trust begins in the team. But again, I will explain how we do that. But trust is critical for a team to operate as a unit and to commit team members to ask questions of others if things are unclear. If I'm a team member and I'm not sure about something, I turn to the team member beside me or I talk as a group, say, Hey, guys, I'm a little unclear on this. You are never, never hesitant to admit that you're unclear about something.

That's what the team's about working together and teams only take on what they know they can complete and they do not over commit. That is a critical part of it. You take on what you can complete and we'll talk about how that is done. So that is the first value, how it's achieved. Now we're going to look at it from a scrum master perspective. How do scrum masters work with this? Well, they reinforce the commitment of the team during the facilitation of ceremonies. They are the facilitator of every ceremony, i.e. the daily scrum, and they're ensuring that everybody is focused on what the scrum plan has laid out, what their scrum planning session is, and they're ensuring that during each day that the team is committed to achieving that end result of their issues. They talk about it, but that is where it is. Enforce that commitment.

And the scrum masters protect teams from mid sprint changes, you say, and you say the product owner can make changes whenever they want. Yes to the product backlog, not to the sprint backlog. Once the sprint backlog is chosen, you work with it and finish that sprint backlog. Yes, you may have to make some changes, write up new uses stories and put those into the next sprint or future sprints. But once the team commits to the sprint, that's the work that's done. And the scrum master keeps the commitment of the team to make sure that the team meets its commitment, deflects pressure from stakeholders who want extra changes, they want this to change.

No, you deflect that and have the product owner handle that. That's what the product owner is for. So that is what we call the commitment value of the team. The second value that we look at is courage. The team values courage. And how do they do that well? What is courage? First of all, it is mental or moral strength to venture, to persevere and withstand danger of fear or difficulty, which we have on all teams in product development. So the team commits to working with how well, first of all, teams must feel safe enough to do what to do this to say no. To ask for help. To try new things takes courage, and this is what is encouraged on teams to actually step out and do this to grow this value of courage and to question the status quo when the status quo negatively impacts their success.

Well, this is the way we've always done it. If that's going to impact my success negatively, I will question that the team will question it. So this is what the team focuses on. And from a courage perspective, what does the scrum master do? Well, they create a safe environment for teams to have those difficult conversations. And it's just not saying we'll go and have a conversation, it is encouraging, it is. That's part of the scrum master roll. We'll talk about it as a servant leadership role to encourage them to come to draw them out, and there are questions that can be asked to draw this out. You need to have conversations with team members, with stakeholders, with the product owner. And be fearless about removing impediments.

Every every daily scrum we have the opportunity to have our impediments laid out. The scrum masters role is immediately after the daily scrum to begin working on removing those impediments and be fearless about it. If it means going to the CEO and saying we need to have this changed or we need this stakeholder to step out of interfering. Then you do it. That is the critical part of it and to stand up to stakeholders, no matter how high up the organizational structure they are. It takes courage to do that. And then when priorities shift, adapt, don't be too proud. Have the courage to adapt to those shifts in priorities. So that's the value of courage. Number three is focus, a point of concentration every sprint that we do. We focus on keeping the team focused on getting that complete what we have committed to.

So from a team perspective, we say this. This is one of the best skills for the team to develop in our culture today, there is so much noise. There are so many distractions that pull people from focus. So this is a tremendous skill that you have that the team can have to keep focused on what they have committed to. And again, focus takes courage as well. Whatever you start, you finish, whatever the team starts, they finish and the team is relentless, relentless about simplicity, and that is maximizing the amount of work not done. If we spot something that we feel will not be used in the system or we get the message from the product owner, what we don't know, we're going to be relentless in getting that eliminated from the system.

Now the scrum master, from a focused perspective, what do they do? Well, they hold the team to the definition of done. What is the definition of done well for a user story? The definition of done is the user acceptance criteria. When a user story is developed, the team asks, they use the product owner. What does this story have to do for you to say it is complete? That is written up as our user acceptance criteria or what some of us say the conditions of satisfaction for completion of it. That is our definition of done in scrum masters. For every user story, you hold your team to make sure that everything that is in those acceptance criteria has been completed because the product owner will test it. And if they don't check it off, then we have not stuck to it.

So hold the team to the definition of done and during the daily scrums, ensure only three questions are answered. I know our current or new scrum guide says you don't have to ask those three questions as long as you find out. Have the team members tell you what they worked on the last day since the last sprint, what they will be working on before the next daily scrum? Not the last sprint? What they've worked on since the last daily scrum and what they will work on before the next daily scrum and what impediments that they have facing them. If you've got other ways of doing that and doing it all within 15 minutes of your team, fine, do it. But I find new teams, they go right off track and suddenly there's rabbit trails.

And without realizing it, the scrum master looks at his or her read, and an hour has gone by and a daily scrum should never take more than 15 minutes. If it is, then the process is broken. Scrum Masters takes it. Only insure or ensure only completed work is shown at the Spring Review. We don't mind partial work. We show that we've committed to and we complete, but we've committed to. If it isn't completed, we do not show it. And that is a scrum master responsibility. We're focused on getting done what we committed to. Value for openness. From a team perspective and from a scrum master perspective, openness is the quality of being honest and not hiding information or feelings. That's not easy to do.

And with the new team, it's not going to happen. That's why I encourage scrum masters. I trained them. I work with them. I coached them to draw this out from the team, draw honesty, and don't hide feelings. If there's something that's bothering you, bring it out. And again, it's a real skill for scrum masters to be able to do that. So openness, let's talk about it from a team perspective for team members. It means consistently seeking out new ideas. We're open to doing something new. We've always done it that way. What is the best way? There might be a better way to do it. And when team members grab on to this until it is an eye opener, how things improve the excellence in the product. Just from them looking for new ideas and being open and having the scrum master encourage it and looking for new learning opportunities.

While let's try, this is something we haven't done, it looks like it'll work. And then when you need help, ask. We have this thing called eagle screws up a lot of guys and women too. Well, I don't want to ask, people might think I'm not so smart. Well, they'll think you're not so smart when you screw it up because you didn't ask. So ask when you need help, ask and scrum masters facilitate the openness. That's your job. Try it out. Ask questions in sprint planning. Draw things out. Ask the specific members. Create that environment where they talk and collaborate, where they communicate, and you facilitate openness and spirit reviews by the stakeholders, you get the stakeholders express themselves.

And again, that takes a skill and ability, facilitation is a skill. It's a critical skill for a scrum master, so remember that when you take your PSM one and you focus teams on shortcomings as early as possible. If there are shortcomings, get that out on the table. Facilitate openness in sprint retrospectives, oh, this is a big one, sprint retrospectives, what went wrong, what were the challenges? We're going to talk about how people don't necessarily feel comfortable and you need to get them to be comfortable because how can you improve something if it's not admitted that it's a problem? So scrum masters, it's a big job for openness. And finally, the fifth one is respect. A strong feeling of approval of somebody or something because of their good qualities or achievements.

Let's talk about it from a team perspective, team members must respect all other team members. Don't tear down another team member. Otherwise, you become a barnacle and a good scrum master to ensure that you get scrapped off the team as quickly as possible. Must respect the product owner. Well, the business doesn't work, doesn't know what it's doing, you know you, it is part of your team. It's like a sports team. Sports team members are going at each other. The team is a failure. It never wins anything. So you need to respect the product owner. You need to respect the stakeholders. You're building a product for stakeholders. You're not building it for yourself or for the team or for the policy team or for the financial team.

You're building it for your stakeholders and then team members have respect for your scrum master. He or she is the servant leader, and this is what strengthens collaboration on a team. It is essential. And from a scrum master perspective. Respect the team. And this will generate respect for you from the team. I always tell scrum masters that you begin first. You respect others first and then they'll respect you. Don't wait for them to respect you. So develop respect on the team. How to train teams to listen to each other. And one of the key points here, and I point this out, I talk about in the daily scrum is most people think the daily scrum is about them.

It's about me telling everybody what I'm doing and what my problems are. No, it's about you listening to others and understanding how you can work with them to fix and know what they're doing. Encourage the team to share their struggles and their successes. And facilitate discussions around new ideas and changes to the old ideas. This is a big one. This is sometimes difficult in your environments. If you've been in a long time, change those old ideas and be open to new things.

Do those discussions respect the comments from others? Don't argue and fight because you don't agree with them. So that's what we have in a scrum value perspective. This is straight out of our scrum guide and you'll have access to that. Read it through. But this is what we're referring to in the scrum guide. So that is the chapter that we have on the values in our scrum chapter will end the chapter here. It's gone quite a while, but I wanted to cover all five and one chapter. So this is what we've done and I encourage you. Go back through it, read, listen to it, read the scrum guide and we will see you in the next chapter. Thank you.

What Is The Scrum Flow

And welcome back to the studios of the online Agile Mastery Academy. And welcome back to our core scrum, the master class. So we are in chapter two, which is the scrum chapter, and we're beginning chapter number three, which is looking at what is scrum and answering the question what is scrum which shows you scrum and what shows you the difference between scrum from an overview perspective and our traditional way of developing software. We're going to use that product as our example here. So as we walk into this, this is the process here on the left, we have a prioritized featured list. These are the features that the customer needs, and in our case, we write them up as what we call user stories, and we'll talk about that.

And then we begin our sprint. And you see here we have a small chapter that we extract that we feel that we can build within the constrained time frame that we've chosen, whether it be one week, two week, three week or four week. And then we begin the process and you see that we go through building that software. We've got that smaller ring in the bottom, which is our review on a daily basis. And then at the end of this sprint, we produce new functionality, which is reviewed by the customer or the client. So from a very high level perspective, that is scrum, that's the scrum process. So let's delve into a little more here. One of the things that I always like to emphasize is that the whole focus of Scrum is to help teams deliver value to the customer in small, constrained time boxes early and often.

So we can fail early and often, and we can learn from that and fix early and often, and that's the intent behind it, and it does work. I always like to point this out as well. The scrum framework does not provide answers as to what you should do. And this is a big hurdle for many I.T. practitioners because we like the methodology, which tells us exactly what we have to do. A scrum for the scrum framework does not. It lays out a framework and what that framework will do. It will surface a lot of questions about your organization. Jeff puts it this way, the intent of Scrum is to bring to the surface the problems you are having in building your product or as can, Schwarber says it helps and shows you very quickly where you're screwing up.

So that is the intent. So just to give you some examples of what we mean by that, what the scrum will do for your organization from that said inefficiency perspective, looking at the different inefficiencies a team might have. Using that user acceptance testing process and you leave it till the end of the sprint. We now are inefficient because when we come to the end of the sprint and we do a user acceptance test and the user says, No, that's not what I asked for, which will be the product owner. We haven't met our commitment for that sprint because we've left it till the end. So our process will quickly show that after the first sprint, we have an inefficiency here. Let's look at what went wrong.

And we determine we need to start user acceptance testing at the very beginning of the sprint. I will explain that another typical problem we have with our dysfunctional teams is a number of things. As scrum brings to the surface about dysfunctional teams, for example, team members resist the attendance of daily scrums. I've had this happen and that points out to me that my team is dysfunctional because they think it's about them. It's not. It's about the team understanding where you are and you understanding where they are and what you can work together on to get things done quickly. So if they don't want to be, your team is dysfunctional.

This individual is not a team player, so therefore that brings it out to the surface very quickly. Another thing we look at from a team allocation perspective, and we have a lot of issues with this and many of our matrix styles of organizations where we draw our team together from a number of different silos. You have those people managed by their functional managers within the silo. So you have a time where the functional manager attempts to pull key members off the team temporarily to have them for their priorities. Well, what we've just done is we've failed at meeting our commitment because that person is required for us to meet our sprint commitment. They're gone for two days. We can't meet our sprint commitment.

We are now messed up. It's something that this would bring to the surface very quickly. Another thing that we see our team dynamic issues, scrum brings these to the surface very quickly. We have team members who don't want to work as a team, but they want to be in their silo. We have a developer who wants to sit in a cubicle and just develop and don't doesn't want to talk or collaborate. Well, we have a team dynamics issue here and it comes to the surface within days. And now the scrum master knows what they've got to work on to fix. So we have this efficient flow and efficient team dynamic. There's a lot of things like this that the scrum brings to the surface. It doesn't tell us what to do. It's up to the team to determine what to do.

The scrum is to determine what to do. So that's what we mean by this statement. It doesn't tell us what to do, but it brings issues to the surface very quickly. So let's do an overview between what we've traditionally done and what scrum will have us to do in producing a software product. So traditionally we begin with this waterfall or what we call that relay race approach that Mr Takeuchi and Non-Actor wrote about in that paper. Way back in nineteen eighty six in the Harvard Business Review, they talked about the relay race approach. Well, here it is from the perspective of the way we have traditionally developed software, so we have our stakeholders and our stakeholders come up with a list of requirements.

They're working with a business analyst, they come up with this list of requirements and what they get is a project sponsor to hold the purse strings for the project and a project manager is assigned. So now that project manager will take that list of requirements and determine what they need to build it and come up with a project plan? We have another chart. Once we have that, then this is turned over many times to the VA, the subject matter expert, who will then make sure that they take those high level requirements needs of the stakeholders and come up with detailed requirements, which they then turn over to the architects. We have our data architects who put together our data models.

We have our process architects who put together process models. We have our network architects, we have our security architecture, application architects, technical architects. All of these different silos take that information and add their responsibilities and their requirements to it. And most of those are what we call our in a enough hours or are non-functional requirements. The VA has put together the functional requirements. Now we're putting the non-functional. And then we turn it over to the next silo, which are the devs who feverishly code this. It might take months and they then turn it over to the testers. So we've gone through this silo and the testers at the end have given something to the subject matter expert for the final user acceptance test.

And hopefully at the end we have a product and there we have it. Our traditional waterfall process is done very simply. Well, let's take a look at it simply from a perspective of the framework that we call scrum. Let's look at how that would work with the scrum process. So we end up with the stakeholders putting together their needs and usually working with the product owner to do that. And then we have the team, the team of a product owner, scrum master and developers, that is the team. So with the product owner, they work together to put together the prioritized product backlog and we'll talk about how we do that as a team. It is a very, very interesting exercise.

And then once we have that, we begin sprint number one and we pull out our sprint backlog. So now we have the users stories from the top of the deck that give the most value that the team will work on for the next two weeks. And what will they do? They will produce an increment of working software, which then our stakeholders will go through and review and say yes or no. And if we have to add new user stories, we'll do it and the product owner will set the priorities and so forth. And then we begin the process all over again. So we go through these cycles till we come to the end of the project and we deliver our product. So that's the scrum process. It's a little bit different from the perspective that we work as a team and not in silos, and we do it piece by piece.

The other thing you hear about as we wrap up this chapter is you hear about these two terms that we use, we hear about this one term that we call the committed part of the team or the committed team or the committed people on the project. And you'll hear about the involved people. The committed ones are the ones with their necks on the line. It's not the scrum master who has their neck on the line or the product owner, it's the whole team. They are on the line for the success of this product. The stakeholders are not. They're only involved. And you hear this little anecdote. This is something that we hear a lot of in the scrum and it begins this way. We have a pig in a chicken and they're walking down the road and the chicken says to the pig, Hey, pig, we should open a restaurant.

Pig says, I'm not sure what we call it. Chicken says, Hey, I got a great ham and eggs. The pig thinks and says no things. I'd be committed and you'd only be involved. So therefore we're talking about whose neck is on the line. And that's why we talk about the committed and the involved. You'll find some organizations, they'll call themselves the pigs in the chickens, and some of us, well, I'm a pig on this and some will say, I'm a chicken on this. We will review it. When we go through our in-depth ceremonies, we have a chapter on in-depth ceremonies. We have a chapter from Microsoft in Redmond, Washington, and you hear the product owner call himself a chicken. I'm a chicken on this. So that's where those terms come from.

So that is a high level perspective of scrum, and that's what we cover in this chapter. Now what we're going to do is we're ending this chapter, taking a break, and we're moving on to the next chapter, which will be scrum part one. Now we're going to delve into the detail behind it into this process that we've just looked at from a higher level. I always like to walk through things from what I call a hierarchical perspective. We take a 30000 foot view and then drop down to 20000 and down to 10000 down to sea level and get down to the nitty gritty detail. But we start with a high level picture so everybody can grasp the context. And I find that works the best. I've taught that way for 20 years and it's been always successful, so I'm doing it here. So with that said, thank you. I recommend you go back and listen to this chapter to grab on to this scrum process. And once you have it, then you'll be ready to dive into the detail which we begin and our next chapter. Scrum part one We will see you there. Thank you.

Product Definition

Welcome back to the studios of the online Agile Mastery Academy. And welcome back to our Book scrum, the master class. What we've done so far is we've moved into the scrum chapter of our Book and we've started talking through it. In this particular chapter, we are going to begin to drop into the depth and detail. We're going to do a deep dive, as I like to say. And there's a series of parts that we're going to work through and this is scrum part one. So let's take a look, and I'm going to use this particular graphic that I have produced and used for a number of years. I've updated it, obviously during the time frame, but this lays out a particular view that a lot of I.T.

people can grab a little bit better because it would seem to be more linear, so it lays out the different phases. However, it's not linear other than the front and the back end. So what we have here is this chapter that we call iterations and what iterations are. That's the core part of Scrum that we have always heard about. That's where we get the four ceremonies of Scrum. That's where we get the building of the software. But to build software, you need something happening prior to you dropping into iterations and to release software. You need something after your iterations. The iterations are where you're building your software. Sprint by Sprint. How do you get there? And let me lay something out here. We have a front end that requires us to actually do some planning.

We call it scrum planning and I'll talk about that. That is something that was actually laid out for us way back in two thousand and three and four when I took my certified scrum master education and testing from the scrum alliance. They talked about this front end workshop as you'll hear many people talk about, and they called it scrum planning and we've carried it on. Many of us have carried that on as a front end ceremony and as well there is prior to that, something about laying out the vision, the Northstar of our product. And this is something that's been missing in this scrum guide. Thankfully, in this 2020 scrum guide, we now have it.

We don't have instructions as to how to do it, the scrum guide says. You need it. You need to have your, as they put it, your product goal. What is this all about? Well, we've. Broken that explains that laid it out a little bit better. And this has worked perfectly, I've actually done this ever in the lab for the last 20 years for every project. It has been a tremendous help. And when organizations that are failing see it, they realize that's one of the reasons why we're failing. The other thing that we have is this whole release portion. Many of our projects have a number of releases during the Book of the product building. And again, we don't necessarily have that view in this iterations process that comes after the iterations process. So we've laid something out for that as well.

And as well, how do we deal with it in the production arena? We have changed. So we see here the Black Line goes back to the periodic backlog. We're always keeping that product backlog alive and then we'll move back into iterations. So it's a continual flow moving back and forth. So I want to break that down for the next couple of hours as we talk through scrub and look at what's happening here. Let's deal with the iterations, and that's again what the scrum guide has always focused on, but let's listen to this. I have laid this out and I have emphasized this and this happens in every one of our scrum guys. Scrum is simple.

Try it as is and determine if it's philosophy, theory and structure. Help to achieve goals and create value. The scrum framework is purposefully incomplete. Now this is the key thing here. It is not something that lays out all the instructions, but it is purposefully incomplete. What we're looking at is the links to those incomplete chapters that we have. So if we look here at the iteration chapter, we see where the incomplete portions are and we want to talk about those. This is something that I have called when I'm dealing with different organizations upside down agile. This is where we fail. We've seen this happen a lot in our agile organizations as we're attempting to move that way.

Why is there failure because of this one statement? The scrum framework is purposefully incomplete, and many people move into scrum. Expecting it to be a fully predictive methodology with all the instructions, how to do everything in his canon, Jeff has said Scrum does not tell you how to do things, lays out a framework that will point out where you have issues in building your product, and you need to link that particular framework into your organization and make sure that all aspects are done. So we are dealing with that. That purposefully incomplete chapter and where we want to go is to that first step. This is what we do when we begin the project. We call it our definition.

You can call it other things. But this is where we lay out the vision, the product goal. So let's go back to the Scrum Guide 2020 and see what it says about this. It says commitment. To the profit goal, the product goal describes a future state of the product, which can serve as a target for the scrum team to plan against. We talk about this as a dream. This is the future view of what the stakeholders would like to see and where is that product going? What's in the backlog? It's in the product backlog. You can actually physically put it in the product backlog or what you can do is you can take that product backlog and ensure that everything that's in there is part of the vision. So the product goal is in the product backlog.

The rest of the product backlog emerges to define what will fulfill the product goal. A product is a vehicle to deliver value. It has clear boundaries, known stakeholders, well-defined users or customers. A product could be a service, a physical product or something more abstract. The product goal is the long term objective for the scrum team, so keep that in mind. It is the long term objective it is. What you're shooting for is where you're headed, and they must fulfill or abandon one objective before taking on the next. So let's talk about that. This is what we're focused on. Where does this happen? Where does it happen? Well, obviously to know your view, to know where you're headed.

You have to do it at the front end. So this is the first step and how do we do it? Well, we put together something that we call the Agile Project Charter. I say that slowly emphasize those words as the Agile Project Charter. So what we have in this document is we have a vision, a project vision. What is the dream of our customers or clients or stakeholders for what this project will do for them? You'll hear the term in many of our organizations says this is the Project North Star. This is what the navigators will navigate to. As we, as they did in the olden days when they sailed their ships, they navigated to the North Star. Well, this is our North Star for the project.

We're going to navigate to it. So we have a project vision, but as well as that vision, we ensure that we put a project mission. This is our mission, what the team is doing now. To achieve the vision, we lay out our current mission to achieve that vision. And that mission is what we're continually following as we're moving through the process. Then what we do is we lay out the goals to achieve the mission. And we lay out objectives to meet the goals. So now we're breaking things down finer and finer. And as well. One of the things that we include here is what is initially in scope and what is initially out of scope. And I emphasize the word initially here because this is not a cut in stone document.

This is a document that will emerge as the product emerges when we need to add things to the scope or take things that we do with the proviso in mind. If we add to the scope, something has to come out because we are working with the time box and the dollar box, and we'll talk more about that because that's critical for our projects. So this agile project charter is what we are focused on. And I always like to lay it out this way. How do we build this document? Well, it's a team build. This has to be built with your team, so you've got your project sponsor. You may have a couple of the senior executives involved during this process. You've got your project donor involved and you have the rest of the team, the scrum master and the development portion. They all have to be involved in this process because they have to understand what they're building towards.

Not like the old ways of doing things where everything would be laid out and then it was given to the team and the team didn't have an understanding. So here we have a discussion that goes on. And as I laid out here, how much time it's no greater than three days, it usually takes me with the teams that I coach or the teams that I lead as a scrum master because a scrum master facilitates this. When I lead it, it never takes more than three days, usually about one to two days, one and a half days to actually do this. And you don't need to take time to get it all signed off because the key players are in the room going through this discussion. It is amazing how much time this saves and how everybody is on track.

The questions come up. There is an actual process and I have a Book that leads you through a process of how you define what you're going to talk about, who's going to come in and how long it should take. What are the things that different rules are going to be responsible for? We lay all of that out, but this happens. And how often is this document reviewed, as I mentioned, is not cut in stone. It is something that we review every sprint portion of. For example, when I run a project as a scrum master, as we begin our sprint planning session, we always go back and lay out the vision. Let's keep it in mind. Here's the mission to get to the vision, and then we begin our planning for the sprint, keeping in mind that everything must be focused on that vision.

And remember, in sprint planning, we always begin our sprint plan with a sprint goal. And that sprint goal must be aligned with the mission and vision of the project. So that's how we're an alignment mechanism that we use. That was at what I say here is at the bottom. This equals success. This keeps the team on Book. You don't want to sink the ship. In other words, sink the project because things go off beam. Things go in the wrong direction. This is what keeps us on track. Believe me, I have done this every project. It has been probably the lifesafer of so many projects going back to this agile project charter, which has taken us two days at the front end to build and keeps the team on track.

I will mention this one of the chapters in that charter is what we call the team's social contract. This is where the team lays out what they're going to be responsible for, and we'll talk about that later. So that's where we begin this process, we begin it by laying out our direction where we are going to be going and. That gives us a good fair. Direction and a mechanism to keep the team on track. So that's it for chapter two. chapter number three and chapter two scrum part one, we're going to move to scrum part two. Now is our next chapter. But before you go there, I recommend that you go back and read this and make sure that you have a good understanding of it. And once you have, then we'll move to the next part, which will be our scrum part two. So this is our chapter. Break and gain review this and thank you very much. We will see you in the next chapter. Thank you.

The Scrum Team

Welcome back to the studios of the online Agile Mastery Academy and welcome back to our current Book, which is Scrum the master class. We're in our second chapter of the Book, which is an in-depth dive into scrum, and what we're doing is moving through chapter number four now, which is scrum part two in that deep dive. So we're going to spend a little bit of time in this particular chapter looking at the scrum team. Now I want to emphasize we're not going to go into depth with the rules we do later on in the Book. But what I'm attempting to do here is to give you a quick overview so you know the names of the rules because we're going to mention them over and over again as we go through the different segments of Scrum.

So I want to give you that overview now and then as we get through to the end of the process, I want to do a deep dive on the rules. So you have a good understanding of those rules because you need to know that to write your piece and one exam. So let's go through quickly and look at the rules. Now I want to emphasize that we are not rule focused as scrum. We are goal focused. And what do I mean by that? What I mean is that everybody on the team will do whatever it takes to reach a commitment by the end of the sprint in scrum. What we commit to at the beginning of the sprint, when we do what we're going to call sprint planning and we'll talk about that shortly.

When we do, our sprint planning is to set a sprint goal. The team chooses the work they're going to work on and that choice is a commitment to complete it, to finish it, to make it what we're calling what we call in scrum dun dun. Which means it's not just a system test, it is user integration tested before the end of the sprint and we get a yes or a no. That's our commitment. Our commitment is to complete everything that we start with. So we won't overcome it. But if we are partway through the sprint and we have an issue, the team will swarm on that issue. No matter what their role, you'll get programmers who will be helping testers, you'll get scrum masters who will help the devs and actually do part of the dev, which I've done as a scrum master.

You'll get business analysts working with testers, some of them who've got some experience programming will program. When there's a problem, the team swarms, they drop their roles. It's just like a sports team winning. The defensive team in American football takes over the ball. Someone fumbled on the offensive side. No, the team doesn't just stand around and say, Well, we're not halfbacks, we're not know. Whoever is around there will pick that ball up and we'll head to the end zone of the opponent. They changed their roles. The defensive half backs now become blocking backs. They become blocking lanes. But everybody will adapt and adjust because they're not role focused, even though they've got raw skills that are why they're on the team, but they're focused on the goal.

The goal is to win the game at any cost that is legal, that meets the rules, that doesn't break the rules. Same with us in this on the scrum team. So I emphasize that we're not role focused, even though we've done roles as subject matter experts, but we're going to do whatever it takes to win the game, to meet our sprint commitment or spread goal. So as we talk through that, here are the roles. We have a scrum master on the team, we have a product owner on the team, we have the builders, the developers on the team and that's it. Three roles. Only three roles on the team. Let's quickly talk through them and then we'll dive in in more depth later in the Book we have the scrum master.

That role is the leader of the team and will go to an overview from the Scrum Guide 2020 and then we'll go back into it later on. But the scrum master is accountable for establishing scrum as defined in the scrum guide. You need to know the scrum guide. So for those who are taking the PSM one, all my students, I always recommend that they go through that scrum guide. It's not a large reed. The 2020 version is 13 pages. Go through it at least 10 times, know it inside and know. Be able to quote it if you can. So the scrum masters are accountable for establishing scrum as defined in the scrum guide, they do this by helping everyone understand scrum theory at scrum practice, both within the scrum team and the organization.

So it's just not where my focus as a scrum team knows your focus as a scrum master is the entire organization. It is a hefty responsibility. It's just not doing charts and telling everybody what to do. That is not part of scrum. So Scrum Master number one, and I'm going to go back to the scrum guide 2017 because this is not in the 2020 version. But it is really important that I feel we've all talked to Jeff and Ken about this, that this should have been in the 2020 version, so we might see a change shortly. But the 2017 scrum guide says this: The scrum master is a servant leader for the scrum team. The scrum master helps those outside the scrum team understand which of their interactions with the scrum team are helpful and which aren't.

The scrum master helps everyone change these interactions to maximize, and the key term is to maximize the value created by this scrum team so they're creating value. Each sprint scrum master's responsibility is to ensure that that value is maximized, and the key in this particular paragraph is what I have underlined servant leader. Many people kind of leave that out. It is probably the greatest skill that any scrum master can have and greatest understanding. It is a totally different way of operating, and I have an agile leadership Book that goes in-depth into this because agile leadership is taking over the executive teams in many of our Fortune 500 companies. They are taking on this concept of servant leadership and that's what I train people in.

But that is one of the key skills, if you want to call it, are attributes that a scrum master has is they are servant leaders, and we'll talk about that servant leadership later on in our Book. Then we have the product owner, the product owner. This one individual, and according to the Scrum Guide 2020, the product owner is responsible for maximizing the value of the product resulting from work of the development team. So we're talking about the entire team, but there is a development group within the team, it's not a separate team, so keep that in mind. And we've kind of struggled with this and talked to Jeff and can be careful with this because many people construe it as well. We have a development team and then we have a product owner and we have a scrum and we have a scrum team.

So I like to put it this way. The product owner is responsible for maximizing the value of the product resulting from the work of the developers on the team. How this is done may vary widely across organizations, scrum teams and individuals. So here we go. It's not one way of operating. It varies widely. The product owner is the sole person responsible for managing the product backlog. They own that product backlog. It's theirs. That's why they're called the product owner. So they are responsible, not the other stakeholders. They represent other stakeholders, but it's their responsibility to manage that product backlog. And we'll get into that as we go through the different ceremonies later on in our Book.

Finally, we have the builders, the developers that include testers, program architects, anybody who's responsible for building that product. So the scrum guide puts it this way: developers are the people in the scrum team that are committed to creating any aspect of a usable increment. Each sprint, the specific skills needed by the developers, are often broad and will vary with the domain of work. So they are. The skills are broad because we'll have programmers, we'll have backhand programmers, we'll have front end programs, we'll have user specialists, we'll have application architects, we'll have data architects, technical architects, network architects, security architects.

These are all individuals that come on to the team, and I'll talk about how our teams are set up. We also have, by the way, a

Book just on the team itself and talk through all the nuances of the team and how you bring the team up to what we call a performing team. So this is the scrum team. This is what we will be referring to and always keep in mind that the team is not role focused even though they have roles, but their goal focused. So that's it for this chapter. Go back to it and make sure you have a good understanding of the high level of these roles and know the roles, just know what their roles are. We'll delve into them a little differently later on in the Book. So that's it for a chapter for scrum part two. Now get ready for chapter number five, which is scrum part three. We will see you in that chapter. Thank you.

The Scrum Plan

Welcome back to the studios of the online Agile Mastery Academy. And welcome back to our Book scrum master class. So we are in chapter two, which is the chapter that we're really dealing with scrum and we are in chapter five or we're doing a deep dive and we're beginning scrum part three. So what we're going to look at is, first of all, we've got a series of chapters. We've got the iteration portion, which are the main or the four ceremonies that are traditional. Then we have our scrum planning. We have a definition which we've talked through where we lay out our agile project charter and we have our release and we have our production portion. Well, we are going to focus right now on scrum planning. So we've talked through coming up with our agile project charter.

And now what we're going to do is this next chapter which we'll talk about. So when we look at the original scrum ceremonies that we've had listed for us for a number of years, we see it in our current scrum guide. We hear about sprint planning. We hear about Daily Scrum, the daily stand up. We hear about the Sprint review and finally, the Sprint retrospective. So is that all there is from a ceremony perspective? Well, most of us who've been involved for many years realize there's more to it than that. We begin in this case with sprint planning. This is the creation of the sprint sprint backlog. So let's talk about that. What is required for that scrum guide 2020? Is this the sprint backlog, which is what we're going to put together in the sprint planning session is composed of this sprint goal. That's the way the set of product backlog items selected for the sprint.

This is the what as well as an actionable plan for delivering the increment. How not just what I have outlined there and read. You cannot put together a sprint backlog unless you have a product backlog. You are choosing items from the product backlog. So the question is where does that product backlog come from? Well, many people that you talked to will say, well, the product owner will put that all together. Well, in the ideal world, that might be the case. But in my 20 years in all the organizations, and if you go over to my academy site, you'll see a number of the logos of companies that I've worked with from a scrum agile perspective. I have yet to find a product owner who is a quote true product owner, one who's been trained as a product owner, one who's worked as a product owner, one who understands what this is all about.

That doesn't happen. Usually somebody is assigned as a product owner. Well, they're not going to be able to put together quote the uses stories that are required for agile. I was calling one organization where we actually began the project and they spent eight months putting together requirements. Well, when I walked in within a day that was all thrown out and we began from scratch. So what took them eight months to capture requirements? We built the entire project conformance. So it's not. Pulling together something that somebody has laid out in the list. This is a specific thing that we go through putting together the product backlog, and I want to talk about that. So in the Scrum Guide 2020, it says that the product backlog is an emergent ordered list of what is needed to improve the product.

It is the single source of work undertaken by the scrum team. The scrum team is only going to focus on that product backlog. So we've had a business analyst who's had no experience from this agile or scrum perspective put together a traditional list of requirements. It's not going to work. So the product backlog items that can be done by the scrum team within one sprint are deemed ready for selection in a sprint planning event. So it is an emergent ordered list. In other words, you're not going to get all the requirements up front, you're going to get enough to begin working with and the rest are going to emerge. We'll talk more about that.

I want to go to what has been written from the perspective of what some of us call the scrum planning ceremony by a gentleman by the name of Mike Cone from Mountain Goat Software. Mike has been around since the beginning of Agile. He's considered one of the top trainers in the world today. Everything that we deal with, he knows this is a man of knowledge, and he shares a lot with very large organizations globally. So Mike said this. And listen to this. Read it through in your Book. The agile product backlog in scrum is a priori authorized features list containing short descriptions of all functionality desired in the product.

Now listen to this when applying scrum, it's not necessary to start a project with a lengthy upfront effort to document our requirements. So here's where it comes in. Typically, now this is what is typical for success. A scrum team and its product owner begin by writing down everything they can think of for the agile backlog prioritizing all the needs. The scrum product backlog is then allowed to grow and change as more is learned about the product and its customers through the discussion and to the building of the product. A typical scrum backlog listen to this comprises the following different types of items features. Traditionally, this would have been called functional requirements, but we also have bugs, technical work, knowledge acquisition.

These are the innovators, the non-functional requirements. We need them all. We can't build a system just on functionality. We need to have what the technology is behind it. So the point that I'm bringing out here is it's typically a scrum team and a product owner who put this together. And this is what I have discovered is the most successful way to do it and have used it since the beginning. I was told to do it this way by the scrum alliance when I had my certification for my CSM, a certified scrum master certification back in the early 2000s. This is how they laid it out, that it should be done. I know they've changed it since then, but this is how they laid it out.

So with these are the scrum ceremonies that most of us use. Scrum planning is what we've just talked through, putting together the product backlog and two more items, and we'll talk about that in a minute. Then we have sprint planning, then we have our daily scrum. And in the middle of the sprint, we've added backlog, grooming, refining our backlog and then we have the traditional. Sprint review and Sprint retrospective. So those are the scrum ceremonies that we are going to talk about. So first of all, let's talk about this scrum planning ceremony.

What is going to happen here? What is the process? So this is this area where we've got our charter together. We've got that team together. We know what the business is looking for.

Now we get together the team and it's just the team essentially is all a product owner may call in one or two stakeholders during this session. I always say that this session should never, never, never take longer than a week with me. It's usually two to three days. And we begin programming after that point in time. We spent two days putting together the Agile Project Charter. We spend three days putting together the initial product backlog, and the next week we begin programming, begin our sprint. So that's how quickly it can happen and should happen in a scrum project. So this is the picture I'm going to use of scrum. Scrum is always iterative. Everything we do within scrum is iterative, so we are going to move through this particular graphic over the next couple of hours as we walk through what is happening.

So as you see here, what I've laid out scrum planning, we are producing the product backlog. So this is what we want to talk about. Now I want to say this when I again got my scrum master certification from the scrum alliance, this is what we were taught there. They called it scrum planning. There was a scrum planning ceremony up front. So we know that we have to put it together now. Jeff can have always taught a workshop, a user story workshop. This is where the team comes together and produces the product backlog. So this is why both Ken and Jeff have said this scrum has been left purposefully incomplete. This is for the different organizations to put in place that workshop how they want it done, what they want done, but they need to have it done. It's essential to have scrum run properly.

So this is what we're focused on in our scrum planning. We are going to deliver this initial product backlog. And you see in the initial product backlog, we have a set of priorities and we have estimates relative sizing. These are not hours, days, months or weeks. This is a relative size and we will talk about that. So this is what we came up with in that first ceremony. Scrum planning and there are three products that we deliver. We deliver the product backlog. The product roadmap. And the technical roadmap, it's a technical roadmap, yes, I will explain this, so this is what comes out of that session. So the initial thing we do is we put together the product backlog. This is the to-do list for the system that we're going to build or the product.

What is this? Well, this includes all the needs of the stakeholders. All the needs of the stakeholders are documented here, and what we use is we use this technique called user stories. These are stories. You explain that. The question I always could ask is, why are we using something called stories, why don't we just use our typical standard business requirements? Well, let me tell you something about us as human beings, we are not fact dissemination, which is what a list of user requirements are, just a series of facts. We are storytellers. You think about your life, your life with your family, your community. Go to a sports game. You come back, you talk about it, work. You're telling stories. It's a story.

We are storytellers. So what has happened is Jeff and Ken actually weren't Jeff, and Khanna was Ron Jeffries of extreme programming who pulled that technique into the agile world. So if you want to find out a lot more about user stories, Google Ron Jeffries and you'll see his works. Ron is just an amazing person still out there in the industry. But anyways, he came up with this concept of user stories because we are storytellers. Now the question is, as we look at this, why user stories? And some people say, well, Katie, user stories are producing here documentation no use, a user story is not your documentation. What the user's story is is a key. A key for what was for a door, and that opens the door to what is essentially an agile conversation.

You see, the true need of the customer is not what is written on the user's story, but when they write that user story out in front of the team, the discussion begins. The team begins to ask questions and those questions are going to drive out different things from the user story. And finally, we get the true need of the customer. Just to give you an example, in one of our government organizations, I was the scrum master in leading the team through the process, and we were going through our product backlog and just one user story, the product owner. The way I would work it, they would write down the user story on a yellow sticky and then we would slap it on a whiteboard so they would write it down and explain it. I made sure they always put it off in the corner of the white board.

There's a reason why because as the team began to ask questions, one of the things they used a story always has is on the back of it are the user acceptance criteria. These are the done requirements of the user to say that that user story is done. So in this case, the product owner read off the requirements. Actually, what they did is we wrote those on the wall, on the whiteboard. So there were three acceptance criteria and then the team began to ask questions. Well, as it turned out, we ended up with 17 acceptance criteria that one user story in the term of user stories was now an epic. And from that epic, we grouped those acceptance criteria. We ended up with seven user stories. But that only came out of conversation if we had gone with what the product owner had first written and said, OK, that's what we're going to build.

It wouldn't wouldn't have come close to what the customer needed. So this is what we're focused on. We're focused on that collaboration. But the conversation that comes out of scrum planning brings the true needs of the customer and client to the surface. It is an amazing, amazing technique when done right. You see, we have something in the industry called the Sweetback. If you're familiar with it, put together by the Tripoli Computer Society, the straw man version came out in 1998, and then we had the clay version. And finally, the Iron Man version, as they call it. The final version was in 2002 or 2003. They've had some updates since then, but that is the software engineering body of knowledge like we have in project management.

We have the pin book, we have the Sweetback in software engineering and in that Pemba, it gives us a standard for writing business requirements. And the standard is this. The system must do this. The system must do this well. We're talking about something inanimate, and what we've discovered is that our developers can understand things more when we're talking about real life. So what we do with our users' stories is we come up with a specific format. You might ask, do I have to use this format? No, you don't. But I would suggest that you start with this format because it gets the teams on track. Many of you know that format, which is as I would like. So that we have an actual person, we're no longer thinking about a system. We're thinking about a person that gives a totally different psychological impact here. This is what they would like.

And then they give us the business value. There's no business value. Don't even bother discussing it. So here's an example. As a chief financial officer or as Mary, the chief financial officer, I would like to see our capital asset position so that I know whether or not we can purchase a new asset when the wind that has come available or purchase a new asset that has come available. So what we have here is a story of what that chief financial officer will do when this need is met. So that's the format that we use, and we cover this in much greater depth, we go through all the differences, examples, mapping of it in our use. This story, of course, that we have. So let's look at the product backlog first.

This is the list of customer needs, and we're going to build this in our scrum planning session, so summarization. It is owned by the product owner. It is prioritized by the product owner. Each story is value focused. There must be value to it because this goes along with the principle 10 of the agile manifesto. Simplicity is essential. And what is simplicity, the art of maximizing the amount of work not done. If it doesn't have business value, we don't want to do it. We're maximizing we're pulling that out. And it can be modified continually on an ongoing basis by the product owner, yes, the team can come up with suggestions, they can write out some new user stories, but as the product owner, that will place them in the backlog where their priority fits. So let's talk through it, let's do a scenario here. This is what we do, we first of all in the discussion, we come up with our product backlog.

So this is that user story creation exercise. You might call it a user story workshop. I call it scrum planning, and the team puts together the initial set of users stories once they have enough that we can run. And I usually with my team say, you need enough to be able to work for at least three to four sprints. This might be an entire year's project, but we want to get moving. So we're going to take based on Steve McConnell's own or cloud of uncertainty. We're going to take what we're certain about what's got the greatest business value that we're certain about. We're going to start building it. And then from that we get the team estimate. We estimate in our case here in story points its relative sizing.

And again, we have a Book on agile estimating. So we go through and we lay out the estimates. We have five story points, three story points, one story point. It's all relative to a specific what we call Keystone. We'll talk about that in our other Book. So we do our user story estimation, and then the product owner sets the priorities based on business value. And here we're talking about medium, high or low. Usually, we have a greater spread that allows us to be able to really talk things through. So here we have medium, high, low. I usually like to have a low or medium, low to high, low in a medium or low, medium, medium, medium, high, medium and the same with the high. So it's easier for the product owner to break those out.

So now what we have is we have our product backlog now. The next thing we're going to do is do our product roadmap. We're going to determine our minimum viable product. What from these user stories will give us the minimum either marketable product, the MMP or the MVP, what is the minimum that will give us business value or give the customer value? So again, the product owner pulls in what they see. There's discussion with the team. This is all done with the entire team and we end up with the user stories for our first release. So what we've done to date in that session is we've put together our product backlog and we put together our product roadmap, which is our release backlog. We have two backlogs now we'll end up with a third in a minute.

So the final thing we do is we come up with a technical roadmap for architects. They're looking and listening to the discussion of the user stories. So to actually create that background technology to produce that, this is what we need. So they come together and they will put together the application architecture, the DevOps pipelines that we need, network architecture, security architecture. We also have our whole data architecture. All of this is done alongside the other two items or products that we deliver in our scrum planning session. So there's where we end with scrum planning. We've talked to our definition, which is our agile project charter now we've done the scrum planning our first ceremony.

Now when you're going to write your salmon, I'll talk about this at the end of the Book, you will not be asked about scrum planning. You might be asked about a user story workshop, which you would indicate. This is where you come up with your user stories and you set your priorities and you do your first kind of estimation. So that's it for this chapter. chapter five, scrum part three, go back through it. This is one that you need to go through a few times, so go through it a few times and listen to what I'm talking about. Go into your scrum guide, go through all of that. And once you've done that, we will see you in our next chapter. Thank you.

The Sprint Plan

Welcome back to the studios of the online Agile Mastery Academy. And welcome back to our Book scrum, the master class. We're currently in chapter two, which is our scrum chapter and we're in chapter number six, which is now looking at scrum part four of our deep dive. So far, so far, we've looked at putting together our definition, which was our agile project charter, and then we looked at our scrum planning process, which we went through in depth, the scrum planning ceremony. Now what we're going to focus on, and we're going to take a couple of chapters to focus on this iteration portion. This is the central portion, the iterations that we're doing sprint after sprint, after sprint, the content of our sprints. So remember this scrum planning is done only once at the beginning of the project. You'll do backlog grooming throughout the project, but the sprint planning is, or scrum planning is done once.

So that's that first ceremony. Scrum planning. Now we're going to go into our second ceremony, which is sprint planning. So we go through this iterative cycle that we're looking at, and everything in scrum is iterative, so everything is circular. So we are beginning the main sprint process. So at the very beginning, we go through this ceremony called sprint planning. It is an iterative ceremony and we deliver from that our sprint backlog. This is what we're going to work on in the sprint. So let's go through the process here. Let's begin the sprint. What happens at the beginning? Well, let's talk about that sprint. The sprint, as the scrum guide indicates, we'll read that in a minute. The sprint is the heartbeat of scrum.

This is the core of what we are doing, we are building, we are building, building within the sprint. Let's look at that. Let's read what the scrum guide says. It's got a scrum scrum guy 2020 says these sprints are the heartbeat of scrum, where ideas are turned into value. They are fixed length events of one month or less to create consistency. I recommend much less than one month maximum two weeks. Try one week in a new sprint that starts immediately after the conclusion of the previous sprint. All the work necessary to achieve the product goal, including sprint planning, daily scrum sprint review and Sprint retrospective happen within the sprints. Let's continue during this sprint. No changes are made that would endanger this sprint goal.

We'll talk about this sprint goal, but what we're hearing there is you do not begin to make changes to what you're doing in the sprint, adding things, changing things and we'll talk about that. Quality does not decrease. The product backlog is refined as needed during this sprint, and scope may be clarified and renegotiated with the product owner as more is learned. So going back to that first point, no changes are made that would endanger the sprint goal. We set the sprint goal during the sprint. New ideas come to the surface. The product owner has new ideas or will say, I forgot this and I forgot that. That's fine. What they do, all of that is they write up a New Year's Story, set the priority the team estimates, and it goes into the product backlog. We will not change what we committed to during this sprint. I've mentioned that before and I mentioned it again.

Once we make a commitment, we are going to deliver that commitment. That is our mandate, user acceptance test software and we begin to add changes and take things away. We will never complete what we committed to, so everything is based on our velocity, which we'll talk about in a minute. Let's continue sprints, enable predictability by ensuring inspection and adaptation of progress toward a product goal at least every calendar month when it sprints, Horizon is too long. The sprint goal may become invalid, complexity may rise and risk may increase, which all happens if we have too long of a sprint. Shorter sprints can be employed to generate more learning cycles and limit risk of cost and effort to a smaller time frame. That's why most of us only use a maximum of two weeks.

One week is the best. Try it. Each sprint may be considered a short project. Various practices exist to forecast progress like burn downs, burn ups or cumulative flows while proving useful, these do not replace the importance of empiricism in complex environments. What will happen is unknown. Only what has already happened may be used for forward looking decision making. A sprint could be canceled if the sprint goal becomes obsolete. Only the product owner has the authority to cancel the sprint if you cancel a sprint. We'll talk about this in our chapter where we do a deep dive into all of these ceremonies. This is just the top looking perspective, but yes, we can cancel sprints and if a sprint is canceled, what do you do as soon as that's canceled, you put together a retrospective and you talk about why was this canceled? Understand it.

Debrief, and then you plan and plan the next sprint and begin. You might have to stop it, right? Let's say a quarter of the way through. Well, that's when you begin your new sprint. If it's no longer Monday, then that's fine. Let's continue. Let's look at this happens at the beginning of every sprint sprint planning. So sprint planning initiates the sprint by laying out the work to be fought, to be performed for the sprint. This resulting plan is created by the collaborative work of the entire scrum team. That's the core, that's the foundation. The team, the product owner, ensures that attendees are prepared to discuss the most important product backlog items and how they map to the product goal. So this is why I am whenever I start, we start this sprint planning session.

When I'm a scrum master, we list out their product vision, our product mission and the goals and how the scrum team may, or how this particular sprint goal aligns with that. The scrum team may also invite other people to attend sprint planning to provide advice. Always be cautious, though. With that, you don't want to get the team off track. Sprint planning addresses the following topics. Why is this sprint valuable? The product owner proposes how the product could increase its value and utility in the current sprint. So we want to ensure we've built this so far we've built this. How will that value be increased with this sprint? The whole scrum team then collaborates to define a sprint goal that communicates why the sprint is valuable to stakeholders. The sprint goal must be finalized prior to the end of sprint planning.

Topic to what can be done this sprint through discussion with the product owner, the developers select items from the product backlog to include in the current sprint. The scrum team may refine these items during the process, which increases understanding and confidence. So this is that question and answer thing that comes up. We may find out that in this user story, there's a number of things that we need to add to it. So that will be added. We will estimate that that will happen in sprint planning if this is something that has to be done in the sprint. We might actually find out that this is too big of a user story. It's an epic. We need to break it down. We'll do that. And then two of those user stories can go into this sprint and one in the next sprint, selecting how much can be completed within a sprint may be challenging.

However, the more that, the more the developers know about their past performance. This is critical, their upcoming capacity and their definition of done, the more confident they will be in their sprint forecast. This is why we always maintain the same length of our sprint throughout the entire project because we know that if in the last five two weeks sprints, we are now at a capacity. We were able to complete 25 years of story points or 25 story points in the last two sprints. That's what we're going to plan for this Sprint 25 story points of work. Topic three, how will the chosen work get done? Well, for each selected product backlog item, the developers plan the work necessary to create an increment that meets the definition of done.

Remember, definition of done is the acceptance criteria that we have on the back of the user's story that has been developed during scrum planning and as well during our backlog grooming. This is often done by decomposing product backlog items into smaller work items of one day or less. How this is done is at the sole discretion of the developers, so we don't give instructions or are not told how to do it. We're not told what to do. This is something the developers choose to be autonomous. This is a self-organizing team. No one else tells them how to turn product backlog items into increments of value. Why are they subject matter experts? Very rarely is the scrum master a subject matter expert in programming and the subject matter expert in testing. No, you have experts on your team. Listen to them.

They're going to make the decisions. The sprint goal, the product backlog, items selected for the Sprint Plus, the plan for delivering them are together referred to as the sprint backlog. So that's what comes out of the sprint planning session. Sprint planning is time boxed to a maximum of eight hours for a one month sprint for shorter sprint. The event is usually shorter for two week sprints. My sprint planning sessions never go longer than two and a half to three hours, most times maximum two and a half hours. So what we have is we have sprint planning number one, so we've broken it into two segments and I will explain that. So let's look at sprint planning.

Number one is to go to the scenario here. So what we have on the left hand side is that release backlog. This is what we've chosen for our first release and the team from that to what we just talked to from the scrum guide puts together the stories to meet the product or the sprint goal and comes up with what we have on the right side, the sprint backlog. These are the stories that will meet the sprint goal. Let's talk through the process. So the first thing that the product owner will do with the team once. They have talked through the product vision and product mission and goals. Now we put together the sprint goal, so the product owner will come up with the goal, it will be discussed by the team.

Always keep in mind, make sure that your sprint goal is aligned with your project vision. That's why we bring it up. So we want to make sure that that goal is aligned. So once everybody has a good understanding, then we talk about our team capacity, so we know our capacity. Now, based on the last five sprints, it has been slowly increasing. We should be. We've been at 25 story points, but we think this sprint, we can increase that by two. So we're going to see our capacity is 27 story points. So now user stories are chosen from the sprint backlog to meet the sprint goal and they should meet our velocity.

So we reevaluated our capacity at the end because some of those stories, we may have added more to it and that would have changed the estimate. So we go back through reevaluation and ensure that what is finally chosen will fit our team velocity and that's what happens during part one of our sprint planning session. Well, part two is where we break that down into detail. This is where we do a decomposition, as we say. So the team may define tasks for each user story and we break them down and then estimate those tasks in effort hours. And finally, the team members choose the work they're going to work on. It's their choice if they're not assigned work. We don't have scrum masters who assign scrum masters and not command and control managers.

We'll talk about that. So what we have is this breakdown. Now let me share something here. I don't do this with my teams. Only if you use a story that has three or four different people working on that one story, we may break it into tasks. Why don't I have my teams break them into task? Because what I have a mandate with my teams is a use. A story should never be greater than about three days of work somewhere two days or one day. So what that ensures is we get work completed early in the sprint. The user, the product owner, does user acceptance testing sometimes on the second day of the sprint. We're already beginning user acceptance testing and we've got user stories that small. It is a waste of time to go through and break a two day user story into a task and say, Well, this will take half an hour.

Why I have it done in two days, that's all I need to know. So this is what I work with, but that's super a personal preference. This is something that is personal to me, how I like to see it work. It is just wonderful for my teams, but that's how I work. So again, you as a scrum master with the team, come up with a decision on that. So the first team I ever worked with, with the first three projects, I would always discuss this and say, OK, team, what do we do? None of them wanted to do the breakdown. Now, with teams, I usually say, here's the choice, and this is why I usually go this route. But you make a decision. Nobody ever wants to take the time and effort to break these into my new tasks and do estimating and effort hours.

The reason that this is popular is because it gives a comfort level to traditional developers who've always estimated in hours all this. This gives me comfort. But I'll tell you something: we're very poor at estimating hours. History has shown us. Actually, we feel almost 95 percent of the time when we estimate an hour or time. So I'm cautious about this. I prefer relative sizing, and that way we know that we are accurate. So, Jeff Sutherland, co-founder, I want us to listen to him. What I've done is I've included this short chapter of him talking about the sprint planning session. So let's listen to the Masters. I like to call him co-founder of scrum Jeff Sutherland. So there we have it, chapter two less than six scrum part four, we've talked through the sprint planning now.

This is part of that iteration chapter that I've been talking about, that circular iteration that we're working through. This is the beginning of it. And we've heard our quote, master co-founder of Scrum Jeff Sutherland talking about it. So go back through it. This is one you need to view a few times. Listen to it, go through and look at the scrum guide. I've listed most, most of the scrum guides. The 13 pages are laid out in this chapter. I wanted you to see how it coincides with the scrum guides, so you have a good understanding for your PSM one test, which is what I'm hoping you will take. So with that said, thank you very much for sitting through this chapter and we will see you in chapter six.

www.ingramcontent.com/pod-product-compliance
Lightning Source LLC
Chambersburg PA
CBHW071925210526
45479CB00002B/562